Made *for* More

365 Devotions for the Woman
Who Refuses to Settle

JULIE LEFEBURE

*For the woman who refuses to settle for less
than God's best, and for my Savior, Jesus,
who came to give us life in abundance.*

TABLE OF CONTENTS

HOW TO USE THIS BOOK

This book is meant to walk with you through a year of real life. There's no perfect way to use it—only a personal one. Whether you open these pages every morning, return to them at night, or read when you need a quiet moment with God, let this book meet you where you are.

Each day includes a simple rhythm:

Read.

Begin with the Scripture and devotional reflection. Read slowly. Let one phrase or truth stand out to you. You don't need to rush; abundance is found in attention, not in speed.

Speak Life.

You'll find a short "Speak Life" statement each day. Say it out loud if you can. Let God's truth replace the voice of pressure, fear, or self-doubt.

Talk to God.

Each devotion includes a short prayer to help you begin your conversation with God. You can use the prayer as written or let it guide your own words.

Reflect & Respond.

Some days you'll be invited to journal, answer a question, or simply notice what God is stirring in you. There are no right or wrong answers—only honest ones.

Throughout the book, you'll also find **Reflect Days** and **Rest Days.** These days are just as important as the devotional days.

Reflect Days invite you to pause and look back. You'll consider what God has been teaching you, what has challenged you, and what you want to carry forward. I invite you to journal your reflections.

Rest Days are gentle reminders that abundant life includes stillness. These days are not for catching up or fixing anything. They are invitations to breathe, be present, and receive God's care.

You don't have to start on January 1. You don't have to keep up perfectly. If you miss a day, simply turn the page and begin again. This is not a checklist. It's a relationship.

You may choose to:

✓ Read one page a day.

✓ Linger on a single devotion for several days.

✓ Return to certain pages again and again.

Let this book be a sacred space where you: stop rushing, release pressure, listen for God's voice, and remember what is already true.

You were not made to rush through life.
You were not made to strive for worthiness.
You were made to live grounded in God's presence.

However you use this book, let it gently lead you back to what matters most—God with you, life in Jesus, and the fullness He offers right where you are.

INTRODUCTION

I'm glad you're here. Out of all the books you could have picked up, you chose this one, and that matters. I wrote these pages for the woman who loves Jesus and still senses there has to be more than just getting through the days. My hope is that this book feels like a beautiful space to breathe, to listen, and to remember God's truth about you and about Him. However you found your way here, I'm grateful you did.

This moment from years ago stands out in my mind.

I was in my mid-twenties, driving to work one morning on the Interstate 380 "S curve" through downtown Cedar Rapids, Iowa. It was an ordinary commute; one I had driven countless times. Life was good. Simple. Steady. Yet, as I followed the curve of the road, a familiar longing surfaced again—this time louder than before.

There has got to be more to life than this.

I wasn't unhappy. Nothing was "wrong." But inside, something felt off. I felt like I was moving through life on autopilot—checking boxes, doing what I was supposed to do, showing up where I needed to show up.

I was existing … but was I really living?

Maybe you know this feeling, too.

Maybe you've told yourself you should be more grateful for your life. Maybe you've wondered if this is just what adulthood looks like. Or maybe you've thought, *I don't even know what I'm looking for—I just know I can't keep living like this.*

Quite possibly life looks full on the outside, but inside there's a quiet awareness you can't ignore anymore. A soft whisper that keeps returning. You may not even have words for it yet—you just know something feels incomplete. You know, deep down, there has to be more.

Not more stuff.
Not more hustle.
And certainly not more expectations to meet.

Just … more.

I believe many of us come to this place at some point in our lives. A moment—sometimes intentional, sometimes unexpected—when we realize we're doing all the right things, living the way we're "supposed" to, yet something inside feels unsettled. Not because of our circumstances, but because God is gently getting our attention.

This awareness isn't something to fix. It's an invitation.

God often uses this kind of holy dissatisfaction to draw us closer— to invite us out of merely getting through life and into a deeper, freer way of living with Him.

More depth.
More peace.
More purpose.
More of God.

Jesus declares in John 10:10 that He came to give us true, abundant life. This abundant life isn't reserved for a select few, nor is it reserved for a later time. It's available to each of us now. It's not loud or flashy. It isn't measured by success, comfort, or ease. It is a life centered on God's presence, marked by His peace, purpose, freedom, and love. It's the kind of life that grows softly as we learn to walk with Him, listen to Him, and live from what is true.

When I whispered a prayer that morning on my commute, I didn't have answers, but I began to pay attention. Slowly, God started showing me that I wasn't made to settle. I was made for more—the abundant life Jesus came to give me.

When I say *refuse to settle*, I'm not talking about striving for more or being dissatisfied with the life God has given us. I'm talking about something quieter and deeper—a refusal to live disconnected from the life God is offering right now. A refusal to go through the motions. A refusal to exist without truly living.

Not a perfect life, but a full one in Jesus.
A life rooted in Him, marked by grace, and shaped by His presence.

Decades later, that moment still matters. It shaped the journey that eventually led to this book.

Made for More is written for the woman who loves God but feels tired of striving.
For the woman who wants to live faithfully but feels pulled in too many directions.
For the woman who knows Scripture yet sometimes struggles to live from its truth instead of from pressure, comparison, or fear.

This book isn't about becoming someone new. It's about returning to what's already true.

You don't need to prove your worth.
You don't need to earn God's love.
You don't need to have everything figured out.

You were created intentionally and redeemed graciously—and now invited daily into a life grounded in God's presence. This book is meant to help you slow down enough to remember this—to sit with Scripture, let truth speak louder than your inner critic, rest where you've been striving, and release where you've been holding too tightly.

Some days you'll read a devotional reflection. Other days you'll be invited to pause, reflect, or rest. Every day is an intentional devotion—because living fully with God includes learning when to listen and when to be still.

You are not behind.
You are not failing.
You are becoming.
You are His beloved daughter.

Don't rush these pages. Let them meet you where you are. Let God speak in His timing. Let this be a sacred space where your heart can breathe again.

You were made with intention.
You were made for a purpose.
You were made for a life deeply rooted in God.

You were made for more.

Let's begin—together.

DAY 1

Live Known and Loved

Have you ever felt overlooked or like you didn't quite belong?

Just as God reminded the prophet Jeremiah of how He knew him before he was born, He reminds you of this today, too. You've never been unknown. Never unseen. Not for a single second.

Think about it for a moment: God knew you before He formed you. He knew you even before your parents knew you. He knew what you looked like, what your voice sounded like, even your quirks, and your talents. He knew all of you.

The truth is, no one knows you better still today. God knows you intimately, and because He does, He loves you fully. He's crazy about you and is pleased with the you He created.

Take comfort in remembering how you are completely known and loved today.

SPEAK LIFE: "God knows me, sees me, and loves me."

TALK TO GOD: Lord, remind me, especially when I doubt, that You are the One Who knows me and loves me fully. Amen.

REFLECT & RESPOND: How does the truth that you've always been known by God impact how you live today? How can you pass this truth to another?

DAY 2

Name the Lie and Reclaim the Truth

"We demolish arguments and every pretension that sets itself up against the knowledge of God, and we take captive every thought to make it obedient to Christ."

2 Corinthians 10:5 NIV

What are the false stories you've been believing lately?

Do you believe you're unlovable? Not smart enough? Too messed up? Will never succeed? These aren't just harmless thoughts; they keep you stuck, ineffective, and confused. Scripture tells us to do what with them? *Demolish* them.

Reclaiming the truth starts by identifying what isn't true. A good question to ask today is, "Would God, the One Who created me, say this about me?" If not, eliminate that narrative by naming it and replacing it with God's truth.

You no longer need to be bound by false, limiting beliefs. God wants you to live abundantly. After all, it's the life Jesus came to give you. Because you have the mind of Christ, He empowers you to renew your thinking, speak truth over your life, and live in freedom.

You were created to believe what God says about you.

SPEAK LIFE: "I take my thoughts captive and stand in God's truth."

TALK TO GOD: God, show me the lies I'm believing and empower me to replace them with Your truth. Amen.

REFLECT & Respond: What lie have you believed lately? Write it down, cross it out, then replace it with God's truth.

DAY 3

Ditch the Checklist

"But I trust in your unfailing love. I will rejoice because you have rescued me. I will sing to the Lord because he is good to me."

Psalm 13:5–6 NLT

What if time with God wasn't a duty but, instead, a delight—for you both?

Instead of treating time with God like a spiritual task to check off, what if you approached it as David did: a response to His unfailing love, His rescuing grace, and His goodness toward you?

David didn't worship to earn God's approval. He worshiped because he *knew* God loved him, *knew* God had rescued him, and *knew* God was good. That very confidence stirred joy, trust, and song in his heart.

You bring God joy, too. He delights in your voice, your questions, your laughter, even your silence. Every time you come near, He's already there—not demanding you perform, but rather, inviting you in.

Let today be less about checking a box and more about responding to love. Rest in His goodness. Rejoice in His rescue. Trust in His unfailing love. God delights in time with you.

SPEAK LIFE: "My time with God is a gift to us both."

TALK TO GOD: Lord God, prompt me to spend time with You today—it's not pressure, it's a privilege. Amen.

REFLECT & RESPOND: Understanding that God enjoys time with you, how does this impact you? How does it feel to know that time with Him is a mutual delight?

DAY 4

Bring Him Your Brokenness

"The sacrifice you desire is a broken spirit. You will not reject a broken and repentant heart, O God."

Psalm 51:17 NLT

Have you ever tried to hide the broken places in your life, hoping no one would notice them?

What's broken is often tossed aside or forgotten. We sometimes assume the same about ourselves—that if people saw our flaws, we'd be disqualified as useful or wanted. Yet, God sees brokenness differently.

David shows us God actually invites it. He desires for us to be open, honest, and humble enough to show up as we are, even in the messy, unorganized, and painful places. His specialty is transforming a broken spirit with a repentant heart.

When you bring Him your brokenness, He meets you with mercy. He doesn't discard or reject you, but instead, He restores and rebuilds. The places you perceive as ineligible can be the ones where His grace shines brightest.

Don't be afraid to come to God as you are. In His hands, brokenness is never wasted. It becomes something useful and beautiful.

SPEAK LIFE: "I trust God to turn my brokenness into beauty."

TALK TO GOD: God, I bring my broken places to You. Transform them into something beautiful that You can use. Amen.

REFLECT & RESPOND: What part of your life feels too messy to bring to God? How might you let Him into that space today?

DAY 5

Trust God, Not Plans

"We can make our plans, but the Lord determines our steps."

Proverbs 16:9 NLT

Have you ever had a plan that didn't turn out the way you expected or hoped?

We are a planning-kind of people. We set goals, we dream dreams, and we devise strategies, but Proverbs reminds us it's not you and me; but rather it's the Lord who directs our steps.

This truth isn't saying that planning is pointless. Planning certainly has its place in our lives. However, we are prompted to hold our plans loosely, remembering God knows more than we know. He sees the big picture; we don't. His wisdom is greater than ours, His plans are far superior to ours, and His purposes for us are always His best.

Peace washes over us when we trust Him more than our plans. Today, offer your plans to God, and invite Him to guide your every step. You may be surprised by where He leads, but you can be certain it will be good.

SPEAK LIFE: "I trust God as He guides my steps today."

TALK TO GOD: Heavenly Father, I trust You more than my plans. Lead me and guide me today. Amen.

REFLECT & RESPOND: How will you practically trust God instead of your own plans? Take a moment to thank God for His good purposes for your life.

DAY 6

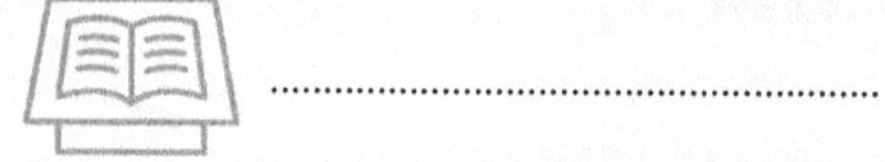

Reflect

Take a few moments to revisit the days you've just walked. There's no rush here—just honesty and grace. Feel free to journal your answers.

Reflection Prompts:

- ✓ What truth stood out to me this week?
- ✓ Where did I notice God inviting me to stop settling?
- ✓ What challenged me? What encouraged me?
- ✓ What thought/encouragement/hope do I want to carry with me into the coming days?

DAY 7

Rest

Today is a day to rest—not to catch up, fix something, or prove anything. Abundant life includes stopping long enough to receive what God is already offering you.

Sit quietly with God for a few minutes.

Breathe deeply.

Allow any Scripture from the past few days to encourage you.

Let yourself be loved and cared for by your Creator.

DAY 8

Care for the Body God Gave You

"Don't you realize that your body is the temple of the Holy Spirit, who lives in you and was given to you by God? You do not belong to yourself, for God bought you with a high price. So you must honor God with your body."

1 Corinthians 6:19-20 NLT

Do you treat your body as a gift from God or as something you criticize?

God gave you your body. It's entrusted to you for your time on earth, to carry out His unique purpose. Yet, we often neglect it and take it for granted. Scripture reminds us our bodies are temples, sacred places where the Holy Spirit lives. This truth helps us see our physical selves differently.

Caring for your body honors the One who made you. Through nourishing food, regular rest, simple movement, or kindly speaking to yourself, you honor God and yourself.

View your body as God's temple, and allow this truth to motivate you to care for it—not out of guilt or pressure, but instead out of love for Him and for the life He's entrusted to you.

SPEAK LIFE: "God gifted me with this body, and I care for it well."

TALK TO GOD: Lord, equip me to care for the body you've given me. Amen.

REFLECT & RESPOND: How does remembering your body as God's gift impact you? What's one way you can care for it today?

DAY 9

Trust in the Lord

"But those who trust in the Lord will find new strength. They will soar high on wings like eagles. They will run and not grow weary. They will walk and not faint."

Isaiah 40:31 NLT

Has life felt unsure, unsettling, or upsetting lately?

Isaiah paints for us a beautiful picture of the one who trusts in God—strengthened, soars high, runs without growing weary, and walks without becoming faint. The one who trusts in God lives a full and abundant life, even through challenging times.

Trusting in God means relying on Him, giving Him our plans and anxieties, and believing His goodness, power, and promises are certain. Even when life doesn't go our way. Even when challenges press in. No matter how our surroundings appear, we trust God will again be faithful. He is in control, and He cares about the details of our lives.

When life feels chaotic and turned upside-down, remember Isaiah's words. Trust in the Lord. He will provide everything you need, right when you need it.

SPEAK LIFE: "Trusting in the Lord is my path to abundant life."

TALK TO GOD: God, no matter what I'm walking through, help me to trust You fully and faithfully. Amen.

REFLECT & RESPOND: In what situation are you trusting God today? Who else in your life needs a reminder to trust in the Lord?

DAY 10

Make Peace
Your Priority

*"Better a dry crust eaten in peace
than a house filled with feasting—
and conflict."*

Proverbs 17:1 NLT

Do you ever assume that more wealth will solve your problems or bring you more peace?

Many people do. Is this what Scripture says, though? It often reminds us of the opposite. An elaborate banquet table may be full, but if it's accompanied by strife, bitterness, or comparison, the feast loses its flavor. It's then not a feast at all. True abundance isn't found in wealth or possessions, but rather in God's peace—peace with Him, with ourselves, and with others.

We experience godly contentment when our hearts are set on God and when we're resting in Him. Living in God's peace can make every experience in life special, even eating a single piece of bread in the presence of His peace can taste like a treat.

Today, be a woman who chooses God's peace over pressure, His presence over possessions, and contentment over constant striving. Your wealth is found in Him.

SPEAK LIFE: "I am wealthy, for I have peace through Jesus."

TALK TO GOD: God, help me to understand that without Your peace, all the wealth in the world is empty and meaningless. Amen.

REFLECT & RESPOND: Where have you been tempted to trade peace for possessions or striving? How can you realign your priorities today to seek God's peace first?

DAY 11

Align Your Thoughts and Words

"May the words of my mouth and the meditation of my heart be pleasing to you, O Lord, my rock and my redeemer."

Psalm 19:14 NLT

Have you ever paused to consider whether your words and thoughts are pleasing to God?

David recognized that the words coming from his mouth originated in his heart. The same is true of us. What we dwell on shapes our words. When we're fixated on fear, frustration, or failure, our speech reveals it. Likewise, when our hearts are centered on God and His truth, our words naturally reflect faith, hope, and trust— the things of God.

Psalm 19:14 isn't a prayer merely about paying attention to what we say; it's about inviting God to align our thoughts and words so both are pleasing to Him. It's a beautiful, transformative, and significant prayer of surrender.

Today, let this verse become your prayer. Ask God to purify your thoughts and guide your speech, so both reflect His truth and glorify His name.

SPEAK LIFE: "My thoughts and words are pleasing to God today."

TALK TO GOD: Lord, align my thoughts and words with Yours and what's pleasing to You. Amen.

REFLECT & RESPOND: What thoughts and words have filled your mind lately? How can you begin to make Psalm 19:14 part of your prayer life?

DAY 12

Give What You've Got

"Each of you should give what you have decided in your heart to give, not reluctantly or under compulsion, for God loves a cheerful giver."

2 Corinthians 9:7 NIV

When was the last time you gave with joy?

God doesn't ask us to give what we don't have, but instead what He's already entrusted to us. Whether it's our time, talents, encouragement, or resources, when we give freely and joyfully, we reflect His own heart. No wonder He loves a cheerful giver!

We are encouraged to give cheerfully, not reluctantly or under pressure. Giving with joy is an act of trust. It declares, "God, I believe You are my Provider, and I know I can never outgive You." When we give with trust, our faith glorifies God.

Your cheerful gift may be the answer to someone else's prayer today. The joy you share in giving will extend far beyond what you see. So don't wait until you feel ready or until you think you have "enough." Give what you have today, and let God multiply it for His glory.

SPEAK LIFE: "I give cheerfully from what God has given me."

TALK TO GOD: God, You've blessed me so I can bless others. Help me to do this cheerfully. Amen.

REFLECT & RESPOND: What does cheerfully giving look like in your daily life? How might God be inviting you to do this today?

DAY 13

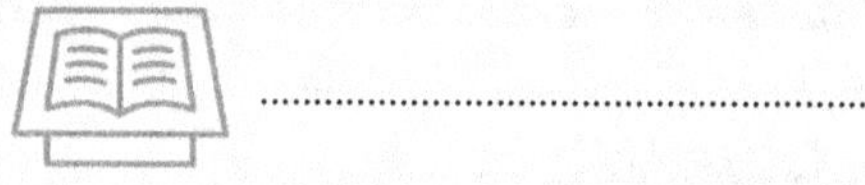

Reflect

Take a few moments to revisit the days you've just walked. There's no rush here—just honesty and grace. Feel free to journal your answers.

Reflection Prompts:

- ✓ What truth stood out to me this week?
- ✓ Where did I notice God inviting me to stop settling?
- ✓ What challenged me? What encouraged me?
- ✓ What thought/encouragement/hope do I want to carry with me into the coming days?

DAY 14

Rest

Today is a day to rest—not to catch up, fix something, or prove anything. Abundant life includes stopping long enough to receive what God is already offering you.

Sit quietly with God for a few minutes.

Breathe deeply.

Allow any Scripture from the past few days to encourage you.

Let yourself be loved and cared for by your Creator.

DAY 15

Do It Afraid and Do It Anyway

"'… Have I not commanded you? Be strong and courageous. Do not be afraid; do not be discouraged, for the Lord your God will be with you wherever you go.'"

Joshua 1:9 NIV

Does the path ahead of you feel uncertain?

Courage is moving forward even when fear is present. God didn't promise that challenges, doubts, or uncertainties would disappear when He called Joshua to lead Israel. Instead, He gave him a promise that He would be with Joshua wherever he went. This same promise applies to you.

It's not a signal to retreat when everything feels uncertain and your mind whispers, *What if I fail?* These moments are invitations to allow God's strength to fill you. Courage is choosing obedience over comfort, trust over hesitation, and action over anxiety.

Doing it afraid doesn't mean doing it recklessly; it means acknowledging your fear while trusting God's presence, provision, and promises. So, step forward. Speak up. Say yes. Allow God's courage to flow through you, even when your own feels small.

SPEAK LIFE: "When I feel fear, I trust God is with me."

TALK TO GOD: God, prompt me today to step forward in what You're calling me to do, even if fear is present. Amen.

REFLECT & RESPOND: What is one thing you've been holding back because of fear? How can you take one step of obedience today as you trust God?

DAY 16

Take Heart and Find Peace

"'I have told you these things, so that in me you may have peace. In this world you will have trouble. But take heart! I have overcome the world.'"

John 16:33 NIV

Where do you look for peace when life feels chaotic?

Jesus never said life would be easy. Instead, He said the opposite: trouble will come. He didn't stop there, however. Peace isn't found in our circumstances, but instead through His undeniable presence.

Notice where Jesus places peace in this verse: "in me." Not in an easy life or in problems disappearing. Peace is based on who He is and what He has already accomplished. The world may feel unstable and full of trouble, but the good news is, Jesus has already overcome it.

No, this doesn't remove difficulty from our lives, but it does reframe it. We are not facing today's challenges alone or unprotected. We are walking through them with the One Who has already overcome it all.

Take heart today. Let Jesus' words settle your heart. Receive peace through Him, and share this peace with someone else.

SPEAK LIFE: "I find peace in Jesus, not in perfect circumstances."

TALK TO GOD: Jesus, when life feels chaotic, help me to remember true peace is only found in You. Amen.

REFLECT & RESPOND: Where do you commonly look for peace? How might focusing on John 16:33 help you receive true peace today?

DAY 17

Remember You Are Wonderfully Made

"I praise you because I am fearfully and wonderfully made; your works are wonderful, I know that full well."

Psalm 139:14 NIV

Are you ever tempted to criticize how God made you?

You are God's beautiful and unique creation. He knew from the very beginning that the world needed your presence, your personality, your voice, and your heart. He purposely chose this generation for you to live.

You are not ordinary. You are a walking, breathing, living reflection of your Creator. His fingerprints are all over you! Every detail—your laugh, your eyes, your passions, your story—was handcrafted with His care.

The God who created the world made you incredibly special, and this reality evokes a holy kind of awe. When He finished creating you, imagine how he stood back and admired His work. You are fearfully and wonderfully made!

The next time you're tempted to compare or criticize what you see in the mirror, pause and remember: God calls His creation wonderful. This includes you. You are worthy of love, care, dignity, and joy—because your Maker says so.

SPEAK LIFE: "God made me wonderfully. I am His."

TALK TO GOD: Lord God, when I forget that I'm wonderfully made, remind me I'm valuable because of You. Amen.

REFLECT & RESPOND: Take a moment to appreciate just how wonderful God made you. Then thank Him today for the you He intentionally created.

DAY 18

Be Reminded: He Never Leaves

"… God has said, 'Never will I leave you; never will I forsake you.'"

Hebrews 13:5b NIV

Do you ever feel alone or unseen?

This comforting verse reminds us that God's presence is continual, not conditional. No matter where we go, what we're walking through, or how uncertain life feels, God's promise remains: He never leaves us. He doesn't step away when life gets messy, nor does He abandon us when we stumble or fail.

Unlike people who may come and go in our lives, God has committed to walking with us through all of life. Nothing can undo this. Even when we feel alone or unseen, His Spirit lives within us. Even when prayers seem unanswered, He is still at work.

When anxiousness creeps in, remember He is near. When loneliness whispers, hear His voice declaring, "I am here." When life flips upside-down, cling to the One Who never changes. His presence is your anchor, your comfort, and your strength. Because He never leaves, you can face today and tomorrow with courage and peace.

SPEAK LIFE: "God is with me always and forever."

TALK TO GOD: Lord, when I feel alone or unseen, remind me that You are with me and will never leave me. Amen.

REFLECT & RESPOND: When have you recently felt God's presence in your life? How can you remind yourself He is near even when He feels far away?

DAY 19

Stop Carrying What God's Released

Do you ever hold on to what God has already let go?

We know God forgives us, but sometimes we continue to replay the past, carry shame and regret, or silently believe our sins still define us. Yet, Scripture says God removes our sins *infinitely* far from us. Not just out of sight, but also out of reach. They are no longer ours to carry.

Think of it this way: east and west never meet. Through Jesus, your past and your present never collide, either. Your already-forgiven-sins are not following behind you, waiting to resurface. They are gone and forever removed. *Forever.*

When God forgives you, He releases you. He restores you. He rewrites your story with His amazing grace—never guilt—all out of His love for you.

Today, stop carrying what He has already released from you. Walk free, forgiven, and clean. Because this is who you are, all thanks to Him.

SPEAK LIFE: "Jesus has forgiven me and set me free."

TALK TO GOD: Lord, because You've already forgiven me, equip me to forgive myself for my sins. They are no longer a part of my life. Amen.

REFLECT & RESPOND: What part of your past still feels heavy? How can you forgive yourself like God has forgiven you?

DAY 20

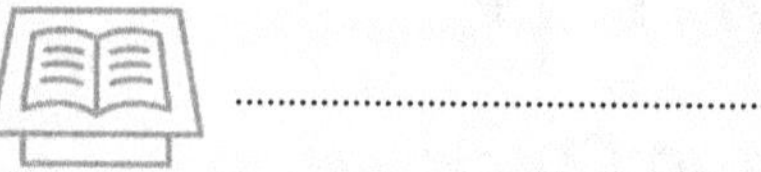

Reflect

Take a few moments to revisit the days you've just walked. There's no rush here—just honesty and grace. Feel free to journal your answers.

Reflection Prompts:

- ✓ What truth stood out to me this week?
- ✓ Where did I notice God inviting me to stop settling?
- ✓ What challenged me? What encouraged me?
- ✓ What thought/encouragement/hope do I want to carry with me into the coming days?

DAY 21

Rest

Today is a day to rest—not to catch up, fix something, or prove anything. Abundant life includes stopping long enough to receive what God is already offering you.

Sit quietly with God for a few minutes.

Breathe deeply.

Allow any Scripture from the past few days to encourage you.

Let yourself be loved and cared for by your Creator.

DAY 22

Quiet Your Heart

*"Be still, and know that I am God!
I will be honored by every nation.
I will be honored throughout
the world."*

Psalm 46:10 NLT

Has life been loud recently?

Voices raise for attention. Headlines scream to be seen. Noises drown out silence and stillness.

Sometimes, the loudest voices are the ones inside us. The noise of worry, overthinking, and what-ifs can drown out the still small voice that reminds us we are safe, seen, and held by our Creator. When we pause, even briefly, to quiet our hearts before God, we are able to know Him more.

This verse isn't simply a call to stop moving; it's a call to pause and remember who God is. Stillness isn't passive. It's a holy space for trust and intimacy with God to grow. It's where His peace replaces the pressures and noises of this life.

A quiet heart knows the One who created it. It's ready to receive and rest. You don't need to do or say anything. Just allow your quiet heart to be still and remember He is here. He's always been here.

SPEAK LIFE: "I choose stillness with God over striving today."

TALK TO GOD: God, quiet my heart so I can know You more deeply today. Amen.

REFLECT & RESPOND: In your day, when can you be still with God? How will you intentionally quiet your heart this week?

DAY 23

Remember, God's Not Finished Yet

"And I am certain that God, who began the good work within you, will continue his work until it is finally finished on the day when Christ Jesus returns."

Philippians 1:6 NLT

Do you ever feel frustrated, thinking you should be further in your faith by now?

Maybe you believe you're falling behind. Or that you're not as far in life as you'd like to be. Paul reveals that the Christian life isn't instantaneous—it's a process. God began His good work in you, and He is faithfully carrying it out.

This means you don't have to be "finished" today. You're not expected to have all the answers or to get everything right. What matters most is your willingness to keep returning to God, moment by moment, one step at a time.

Your journey is made up of many small acts: letting go a little more, trusting a little deeper, following a little faster. Over time, these choices shape you into one who reflects and honors Him well.

Take a breath today. You're a beautiful work in progress, and God's not finished with you yet.

SPEAK LIFE: "God is not finished with me yet."

TALK TO GOD: God, when I get frustrated in my progress, remind me You are still at work in me. Amen.

REFLECT & RESPOND: Where in your life do you feel behind? How could God be working in that space today?

DAY 24

Find Beauty in the Beginning

"'… Do not despise these small beginnings, for the Lord rejoices to see the work begin, to see the plumb line in Zerubbabel's hand.'"

Zechariah 4:10a NLT

Have you ever overlooked the value of a small beginning in your life?

Possibly it felt insignificant, too ordinary, or not worthy of attention. Yet, as Zechariah addressed Zerubbabel, the leader of rebuilding the Temple, Zechariah reminds us that God finds joy in the beginning of the work.

Amazingly, God sees and does what we cannot. He has the ability to grow what feels incredibly small into something far greater—for our growth, the good of others, and for His glory. The seed planted, the prayer whispered, the first step forward—all of it matters and is significant to God.

Don't disregard your start that appears insignificant or small. Celebrate it. Get excited about it. It may feel unimpressive, but it is beautiful to God. It marks the beginning of His work. Trust Him to grow what He's started, and take courage in this truth: He rejoices over every faithful beginning.

SPEAK LIFE: "My small beginning is beautiful to God."

TALK TO GOD: God, help me to adopt the attitude that even a small beginning is important to You. Amen.

REFLECT & RESPOND: What small start is God prompting you to make today? What first step will you take?

DAY 25

Put God First

"One thing I ask from the Lord, this only do I seek: that I may dwell in the house of the Lord all the days of my life, to gaze on the beauty of the Lord and to seek him in his temple."

Psalm 27:4 NIV

What's the one thing you want most?

Is it success, security, or health? Maybe friends, a bigger bank account, or a larger home? David reminds us of what's truly important in life: seeking the Lord above all else.

Our closeness and intimacy with God doesn't happen accidentally—it's a daily choice to put Him first in our thoughts, in our priorities, and in our schedules. When we slow down to spend time with God, we discover that He is more beautiful, more reliable, and more delightful than anything else we could ever pursue.

Abundant life is not about doing, but it has everything to do with being. Being with Him. When your heart is set on God first, everything else finds its place.

Today, before chasing your to-do list or seeking your next big desire, pause and seek Him. Make His presence your "one thing."

SPEAK LIFE: "My desire is to make God my 'one thing' in life."

TALK TO GOD: God, help me to keep you first in my heart and in my day. Amen.

REFLECT & RESPOND: What competes with God for your "one thing"? How can you realign what's important today?

DAY 26

Don't Try to Do It All

"You and these people who come to you will only wear yourselves out. The work is too heavy for you; you cannot handle it alone."

Exodus 18:18 NIV

When have you believed everything depends on you?

We see in Scripture how not even God's chosen people could do everything on their own, including Moses, the leader of the Israelites. He was attempting to judge every dispute, answer every question, and manage every person's needs until his father-in-law stepped in and said what he was doing was too much for one person.

That same wisdom is for us today, too. In a world that praises hustle and a do-it-yourself mentality, God has never asked us to carry every load and meet every demand. When we try to, we end up weary, worn out, resentful, and missing the abundant life.

It's okay to say no and release what's too much. Lean on others, and more importantly, lean on God. You don't have to do it all. Allow God to do it instead.

SPEAK LIFE: "I'm not expected to do it all. I rely on God instead."

TALK TO GOD: Lord God, show me how to lean on You instead of trying to do it all on my own. Amen.

REFLECT & RESPOND: Where are you trying to do it all right now? What might God be inviting you to release?

DAY 27

Reflect

Take a few moments to revisit the days you've just walked. There's no rush here—just honesty and grace. Feel free to journal your answers.

Reflection Prompts:

- ✓ What truth stood out to me this week?
- ✓ Where did I notice God inviting me to stop settling?
- ✓ What challenged me? What encouraged me?
- ✓ What thought/encouragement/hope do I want to carry with me into the coming days?

DAY 28

Rest

Today is a day to rest—not to catch up, fix something, or prove anything. Abundant life includes stopping long enough to receive what God is already offering you.

Sit quietly with God for a few minutes.

Breathe deeply.

Allow any Scripture from the past few days to encourage you.

Let yourself be loved and cared for by your Creator.

DAY 29

Open Your Hands

"And I have been a constant example of how you can help those in need by working hard. You should remember the words of the Lord Jesus: 'It is more blessed to give than to receive.'"

Acts 20:35 NLT

Are you living with open hands or closed fists?

Clenched fists hold on to resources, time, and plans, leaving little room for God's provision or opportunities to bless others. Open hands, however, release freely, trusting Him to supply what we need.

Paul reminded the believers in Acts that helping others is central to following Jesus. Generosity is more than an action. It's a reflection of Jesus Himself. He opened His hands fully, giving His very life so that we could live forever with Him.

Jesus said it's more blessed to give than to receive. The blessing comes in trusting God enough to live open-handed, offering what we have for the good of others.

Today, look for a way to give—your time, resources, or encouragement. In blessing someone else, you'll discover the greater blessing of walking in step with Jesus and His words.

SPEAK LIFE: "My hands are open to give and receive."

TALK TO GOD: Lord, help me live with open hands to You, to give and receive. Amen.

REFLECT & RESPOND: Where is God asking you to give and bless others today? How will you step out in faith?

DAY 30

Trust Truth Over Fear

"Don't be afraid, for I am with you. Don't be discouraged, for I am your God. I will strengthen you and help you. I will hold you up with my victorious right hand."

Isaiah 41:10 NLT

What fear is loudest in your life right now?

Fear shouts worst-case scenarios, what-ifs, and lies that cause panic within us. God, however, drowns out fear with His promises. Isaiah reminds us of Who God is, especially in the face of fear. We are not to be afraid because God is with us.

Fear says, "You're alone."
God says, "I am your God."

Fear says, "You're too weak."
God says, "I will strengthen you."

Fear says, "You won't make it."
God says, "I will help you."

When fear gets loud, we have a choice: to trust the voice of fear or the truth of God. Trust doesn't mean we never feel afraid. It means we claim God's presence instead of fear's lies.

Today, when fear tries to cause panic within you, remember God's victorious right hand is holding you now. You're steadied, secured, and strengthened.

SPEAK LIFE: "God's truth is greater than the voice of fear."

TALK TO GOD: God, help me to trust You wholeheartedly when fear gets loud. Amen.

REFLECT & RESPOND: What fear is loudest in your life right now? How will you intentionally trust God's truth over that fear?

DAY 31

Remember This in Hardships

"For our present troubles are small and won't last very long. Yet they produce for us a glory that vastly outweighs them and will last forever!"

2 Corinthians 4:17 NLT

Are the hardships you're facing today wearing you down?

The truth Paul shares gives us hope: hardships may feel heavy today, but compared to eternity, they are light. The struggles of life can seem long, but next to forever, they are momentary. God promises that every trial is purposeful, and the glory awaiting us surpasses anything we can imagine now.

This doesn't minimize our pain today; instead, it dignifies it. Our tears, sacrifices, and perseverance in faith are never wasted. They are used for something eternal, something glorious. One day, when standing in God's presence, we'll see how every faith-filled moment carried an eternal benefit that we couldn't see at that time. Allow this to encourage your heart today.

When burdens feel overwhelming, remember: they are producing something beautiful and lasting. Glory is being written into your story.

SPEAK LIFE: "God uses life's hardships for eternal significance."

TALK TO GOD: Lord, when I get weighed down by earthly problems, remind me You are using them for something beautiful. Amen.

REFLECT & RESPOND: How does this verse reshape the way you see your current struggles? Where can you lean on God's strength to endure with hope?

DAY 32

Let God Multiply Your Gift

"'There's a young boy here with five barley loaves and two fish. But what good is that with this huge crowd?'"

John 6:9 NLT

Have you ever felt like what you had to offer was too small to matter?

Maybe our time, our talents, or our resources seem insignificant compared to the need before us. That's what the disciples faced with feeding over 5,000 people with a boy's small lunch. Jesus showed them, as He shows us, a kingdom truth: in His hands, little becomes much.

The boy simply gave what he had. Jesus blessed it, multiplied it, and used it to satisfy the entire crowd—with plenty to spare. The miracle wasn't in the size of the gift, but instead in the Savior who used it. When we offer what we have, no matter how insufficient it seems, God multiplies it for His glory and the good of others.

Friend, don't underestimate the power of your "little." In God's hands, it's more than enough.

SPEAK LIFE: "When I give what I have, God makes it sufficient."

TALK TO GOD: God, remind me that nothing is too small for You to use and to multiply according to Your will. Amen.

REFLECT & RESPOND: What small thing is God asking you to offer Him? How are you relying on Him to multiply what you give?

DAY 33

Trust God's Yes

"For all of God's promises have been fulfilled in Christ with a resounding 'Yes!' And through Christ, our 'Amen' (which means 'Yes') ascends to God for his glory."

2 Corinthians 1:20 NLT

When was the last time someone made a promise to you, and then broke it?

This stings, and it prompts us to be hesitant to trust the promises of others. Yes, people break their word, circumstances change, and our own hearts can be fickle, yet God always remains trustworthy. When He makes a promise, He always keeps it. Paul reminds us that every promise God has spoken finds its completion and fulfillment in Jesus.

His "yes" is eternal. It's lasting. Every word He speaks is unwavering, sealed by the cross and confirmed by the empty tomb. When doubts creep in—or life feels uncertain—with confidence, we can believe His promises are true. He has said "yes" to forgiving our sins, giving us new life, and living with Him forever.

Because He is faithful, we can boldly say, "Amen," trusting His promises and aligning our lives with His truth.

SPEAK LIFE: "I trust God and His promises today."

TALK TO GOD: God, thank You for always keeping Your promises. Guide me to trust You through them today. Amen.

REFLECT & RESPOND: Which promise of God feels most life-giving to you right now? How will you live in confident trust in Him moving forward?

DAY 34

Reflect

Take a few moments to revisit the days you've just walked. There's no rush here—just honesty and grace. Feel free to journal your answers.

Reflection Prompts:

- ✓ What truth stood out to me this week?
- ✓ Where did I notice God inviting me to stop settling?
- ✓ What challenged me? What encouraged me?
- ✓ What thought/encouragement/hope do I want to carry with me into the coming days?

DAY 35

Rest

Today is a day to rest—not to catch up, fix something, or prove anything. Abundant life includes stopping long enough to receive what God is already offering you.

Sit quietly with God for a few minutes.

Breathe deeply.

Allow any Scripture from the past few days to encourage you.

Let yourself be loved and cared for by your Creator.

DAY 36

Embrace Your Real Name

"But now, O Jacob, listen to the Lord who created you. O Israel, the one who formed you says, 'Do not be afraid, for I have ransomed you. I have called you by name; you are mine ...'"

Isaiah 43:1 NLT

Think your name is not important?

Think again. In Scripture, names reveal people's identity or calling. They may even signify a fresh start. They tell a story. They matter.

Through the prophet Isaiah, God told the Israelites He called them by name and they were His. This truth applies to you, too. When God calls your name, He's not just identifying you. He's claiming you—declaring you are His.

The world may try to name you unworthy, unimportant, unimpressive, or uninvited. But God names you: beloved, daughter, masterpiece, chosen.

When false descriptors try to sneak in, such as defeated or self-doubting—or how others have labeled you—pause, and remember your true name. God's voice matters the most. You are who He says you are. He calls you His. This name defines you and is the only one that truly matters.

SPEAK LIFE: "God calls me by name. I am His."

TALK TO GOD: God, help me remember my true name and who I am in You. Amen.

REFLECT & RESPOND: What name have you been carrying that God never gave you? Release it and claim what He says about you instead.

DAY 37

Trust God with the Broken Pieces

"He will not crush the weakest reed or put out a flickering candle. He will bring justice to all who have been wronged."

Isaiah 42:3 NLT

Ever think you're too broken for God?

Maybe life has worn you out. Maybe circumstances, choices, or words have left you shattered. Broken dreams, broken trust, broken confidence—they can cause you to feel that it's impossible to ever be whole again.

Here is the truth: God never discards the broken. As Isaiah reminds us, He doesn't extinguish a flickering flame; He protects it. He doesn't crush the weak—He lifts them up and cares for them tenderly.

Jesus came for the bruised and battered, not the polished and perfect. Your brokenness isn't a disqualifier—quite the opposite. It's the very place where His healing begins. He is an expert at working with broken pieces. He reshapes what was shattered into something purposeful and new.

If you feel weak, weary, or worn thin, remember this: He sees, and He cares. You are safe. He holds your fragile places gently, with love. In His hands, even brokenness becomes beauty.

SPEAK LIFE: "God is restoring and redeeming every part of me."

TALK TO GOD: Lord God, please bring healing, wholeness, and restoration where needed in my life. Amen.

REFLECT & RESPOND: In what area of your life do you feel too broken? Invite God into it and trust His restoration.

DAY 38

Come Back Home

Have you noticed yourself drifting lately?

It doesn't usually happen all at once. It's subtle—one distraction, one delay, one hard moment or season at a time. You may not even realize how far you've wandered until you stop and notice the distance. No matter how far you've strayed, there is good news: God is always ready to welcome you back.

Hosea offers a call to return—not out of trembling, but rather, out of love. It's never too late. You haven't gone too far. Even if your heart feels cold or distant, ashamed or unworthy, His heart remains warm and open toward you.

God isn't waiting with an *I-told-you-so* judgment. He's not ready to pounce with punishment. Nor is He disappointed in you. He simply offers restoration. He knows where you've been and what's pulled you away, and still, He whispers, *Come home.*

No matter what's caused you to drift—temptation, hurt, disappointment, or distraction—His welcoming arms are wide open, ready to welcome you back.

SPEAK LIFE: "Even if I've drifted, I can always return to God."

TALK TO GOD: God, thank You for Your healing and restoration. Remind me that my home is with You. Amen.

REFLECT & RESPOND: Where have you drifted from God? Take one small step today to return. He's already waiting.

DAY 39

Live Your Full Life

"The thief comes only to steal and kill and destroy; I have come that they may have life, and have it to the full."

John 10:10 NIV

Could it be that the full life you long for is available to you right now?

The world defines abundance as having more—more money, more success, more stuff. Yet, Jesus defines it in a completely different manner. His abundance is far superior to possessions and greater than circumstances. It's a life characterized by His peace that calms, His joy that overflows, His freedom that restores, and His presence that remains.

The enemy wants to rob you of this abundant life, whispering lies that keep you chasing after what can never satisfy. Jesus, however, came to give you more than survival; He came to give you a life overflowing with Him.

True abundance isn't something you earn, buy, or achieve; it's something you receive in Jesus. The good news? That full, abundant life is available to you today—not someday far off, but rather, right here, right now.

SPEAK LIFE: "My abundance is found in Jesus alone."

TALK TO GOD: Heavenly Father, lead me to keep my perspective on abundance centered on Jesus. Amen.

REFLECT & RESPOND: Where might you be tempted to seek abundance in lesser things? What's one thing you can do to live more fully in His presence today?

DAY 40

Let His Love Motivate You

"So now I am giving you a new commandment: Love each other. Just as I have loved you, you should love each other."

John 13:34 NLT

What would change if love was your motivating factor today?

Jesus doesn't suggest this as His preference. Instead, it's a command. This isn't just any kind of love; it's the kind He Himself demonstrated: patient, sacrificial, attentive, and intentional. Loving others the way Jesus loves us requires more than good intentions; it requires prioritizing love every day.

This kind of love shows up in how we listen, forgive, and respond, especially when it's inconvenient or tiresome. It values others over ourselves, and giving over receiving. When His love leads us, we can't help but love like Jesus. Amazingly, His presence becomes visible through how we love others.

Today, let Jesus' love motivate your life. Allow it to lead you in all you do: how you speak, how you act, and how you respond. Loving others well is one of the most powerful ways to reflect Him.

SPEAK LIFE: "I let Jesus' love motivate all I do."

TALK TO GOD: Jesus, equip me to love others as You love me. May others see You through me. Amen.

REFLECT & RESPOND: Who have you struggled to love well lately? Ask Jesus to transform your heart and to help you love this one with His love.

DAY 41

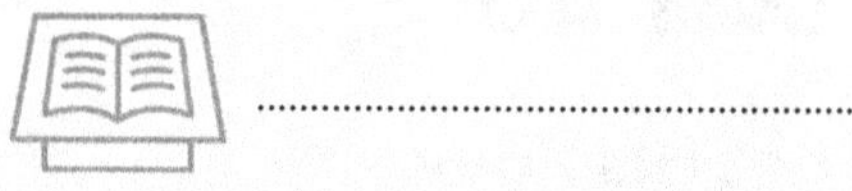

Reflect

Take a few moments to revisit the days you've just walked. There's no rush here—just honesty and grace. Feel free to journal your answers.

Reflection Prompts:

- ✓ What truth stood out to me this week?
- ✓ Where did I notice God inviting me to stop settling?
- ✓ What challenged me? What encouraged me?
- ✓ What thought/encouragement/hope do I want to carry with me into the coming days?

DAY 42

Rest

Today is a day to rest—not to catch up, fix something, or prove anything. Abundant life includes stopping long enough to receive what God is already offering you.

Sit quietly with God for a few minutes.

Breathe deeply.

Allow any Scripture from the past few days to encourage you.

Let yourself be loved and cared for by your Creator.

DAY 43

Stay Encouraged While You Grow

"The way of the righteous is like the first gleam of dawn, which shines ever brighter until the full light of day."

Proverbs 4:18 NLT

Do you ever feel discouraged because growth feels slow?

God doesn't change us all at once, does He? He leads us step by step, moment by moment. Proverbs reminds us that the path of the righteous isn't instant change. It's gradual. Like a sunrise, what begins faint grows clearer, stronger, and brighter with time.

Spiritual growth often feels subtle. You may not notice dramatic changes or immediate transformation, yet God is at work. Each faithful choice, each small act of obedience, each quiet moment of trust adds more light to your path.

You're not behind. You're not stuck. You're growing.

God doesn't rush the work He's doing in you. He knows exactly what He's doing, and as you keep walking with Him, He continues to mold you.

Refuse to measure your growth by how far you think you should be. Trust God's process. Stay on His path. His light is shining through you, even if you can't see it yet.

SPEAK LIFE: "God is at work growing me today."

TALK TO GOD: Lord, when I get discouraged because I don't see growth, remind me You are working within me. Amen.

REFLECT & RESPOND: Where do you feel most discouraged in your spiritual growth? How does remembering Proverbs 4:18 encourage you today?

DAY 44

Let God Lead You

"Whether you turn to the right or to the left, your ears will hear a voice behind you, saying, 'This is the way; walk in it.'"

Isaiah 30:21 NIV

When was the last time you let God lead?

The people of Judah had a tendency to stray from God's path or to seek outside sources for their guidance. Don't we sometimes do the same? Isaiah's promise encourages us with the truth that God leads us in His perfect way for our lives—but will we let Him?

When we are unsure which direction to take or which decision to make, seeking God and His wisdom will always be our best choice. Yet, sometimes we look to other people, or we guess which way to go, forgetting that God is willing and ready to guide us.

Seek God, and give Him the opportunity to be the voice behind you, lovingly guiding you in the right direction and equipping you to walk that way. Allow God to lead you in His perfect will. You'll experience true, lasting, abundant life.

Speak Life: "Seeking God and His wisdom for direction leads me to abundant life."

Talk to God: Lord God, Your way is perfect for me. Help me to seek You and allow You to lead me. Amen.

Reflect & Respond: Where are you resisting God's leading in your life? What can you do today to seek Him and His will?

DAY 45

Trust God's Provision

"But when they measured it out, everyone had just enough. Those who gathered a lot had nothing left over, and those who gathered only a little had enough. Each family had just what it needed."

Exodus 16:18 NLT

Do you ever feel like you don't have enough?

God's provision for the Israelites in the wilderness reminds us that He gives exactly what we need—not always what we want. Some gathered much, and others gathered little. Yet, all had enough. This is the foundation of contentment: trusting that what He's placed in our hands for today is sufficient.

The world urges us to stockpile and chase more, but God invites us into a simpler rhythm of daily dependence. His peace fills us to overflowing when we release the craving for excess and appreciate His faithful provision, even when it looks different from what we imagined.

Today, God has already given you enough—enough grace, strength, and resources. Tomorrow's needs will be met tomorrow. Rest in His care, and let your heart find peace in His provision.

Speak Life: "Today, I trust that what I have is enough."

Talk to God: Lord God, when I'm tempted to stockpile or strive for more, remind me You provide all I need. Amen.

Reflect & Respond: Where do you feel you need more right now? How might God be inviting you to see His provision as enough?

DAY 46

Let the Word Shape Your Words

"Your word is a lamp to guide my feet and a light for my path."

Psalm 119:105 NLT

What fills your heart and mind?

We demonstrate what we are full of by the words we speak. If our thoughts are overwhelmed with fear, frustration, or negativity, our words reflect that. On the other hand, when we are filled with God's Word of truth, we speak accordingly.

Scripture doesn't merely inform us; it reforms us. It retrains our minds to see life through God's perspective, teaching us to bless instead of curse, encourage instead of dismantle, and declare truth instead of lies. The more we read and study His Word, the more naturally it flows out of us in conversations, prayers, and even in the quiet talk within ourselves.

Let your well be filled by drawing from His Word. As you read, study, and speak Scripture, your words will begin to echo His life-giving truth in a world so desperate for hope.

SPEAK LIFE: "God's Word guides my life and the words I speak."

TALK TO GOD: Heavenly Father, prompt me to spend time reading and studying Your Word so my words will be filled with hope, promise, and blessing. Amen.

REFLECT & RESPOND: What Scriptures do you turn to when you need encouragement or strength? How will you allow them to reshape the way you speak today?

DAY 47

**Bless
with Your
Blessings**

*"'I will make you into a great nation,
and I will bless you; I will make
your name great, and you will be
a blessing ...'"*

Genesis 12:2 NIV

Have you ever realized God's blessings were never designed to stop with you?

God's call to Abraham wasn't just about his own prosperity; it was about becoming a means of blessing for others. This principle still applies today.

When you think of blessings, you might picture financial or material resources. Yet, God's blessings extend far beyond these. Time, encouragement, wisdom, talents, and even life lessons you've walked through can all be blessings to others. Nothing God has given you is meant to be hoarded; it's meant to flow from you to others.

God has already given us what we need to bless others. When we willingly offer what we have, God multiplies it and increases our joy in the process.

You are blessed, not by accident—but on purpose. Part of that purpose is to bless others to leave a legacy that impacts those far beyond you.

SPEAK LIFE: "God has blessed me to be a blessing to others."

TALK TO GOD: Lord, open my eyes to see how I can bless others with what You've blessed me. Amen.

REFLECT & RESPOND: How has God blessed you recently? Who can you bless today with what God has already given you?

DAY 48

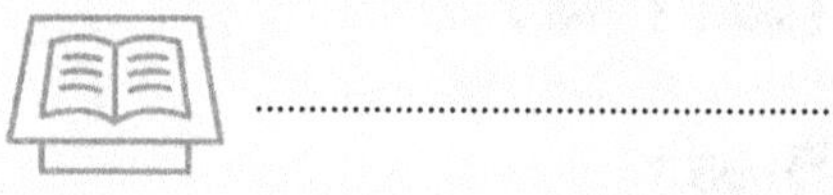

Reflect

Take a few moments to revisit the days you've just walked. There's no rush here—just honesty and grace. Feel free to journal your answers.

Reflection Prompts:

- ✓ What truth stood out to me this week?
- ✓ Where did I notice God inviting me to stop settling?
- ✓ What challenged me? What encouraged me?
- ✓ What thought/encouragement/hope do I want to carry with me into the coming days?

DAY 49

Rest

Today is a day to rest—not to catch up, fix something, or prove anything. Abundant life includes stopping long enough to receive what God is already offering you.

Sit quietly with God for a few minutes.

Breathe deeply.

Allow any Scripture from the past few days to encourage you.

Let yourself be loved and cared for by your Creator.

DAY 50

Offer Your Obedience

"Jesus replied, 'Anyone who loves me will obey my teaching. My Father will love them, and we will come to them and make our home with them ...'"

John 14:23 NIV

When you think about obedience to God, what comes to mind?

Some may think it's restrictive. Others believe it's about following a set of rules out of duty or fear. Jesus, however, clearly states obedience is connected to something else: love.

Our devotion to God and love for Him are what drive our obedience. In return, God responds with His presence. This is the abundance we long for—not for material blessings, but rather for the reality of God Himself dwelling with us. As a result, His love, peace, and power fill the God-shaped hole in each of us.

Yes, sometimes obedience may stretch us, force us out of comfort zones, or require us to release the control we thought we had. Yet, on the other side of obedience is the joy of walking closer with Him.

Every act of obedience you offer today invites God's abundance into your life.

SPEAK LIFE: "My obedience today brings God's peace, power, and presence."

TALK TO GOD: Lord God, motivate me to continually walk in loving obedience to You, even when it feels difficult. Amen.

REFLECT & RESPOND: Where is God inviting you to step into obedience today? How will you respond to experience His abundance?

DAY 51

Look Forward to What's Ahead

"But we are citizens of heaven, where the Lord Jesus Christ lives. And we are eagerly waiting for him to return as our Savior."

Philippians 3:20 NLT

Is life feeling a bit unsettled right now?

May this truth settle in deep: this world is not our home. Paul reminds us that our citizenship is in heaven, not on earth. We are just travelers here, passing through on the way to our forever home with Jesus. The frustrations, disappointments, and imperfections we experience today point us to look forward with hope to what's ahead.

In heaven, every tear will be wiped away, brokenness will be no more, and joy will never end. *Can you even fathom it?* Remembering this steadies us when life gets shaky. It keeps us from placing our hope in earthly things that can fade, fail, or disappoint. Instead, we fix our eyes on Jesus, our eternal King, and live today with heaven in mind.

Home is ahead. It is glorious, and it is yours.

SPEAK LIFE: "My true home is not here; it's with Jesus."

TALK TO GOD: Lord, daily remind me that heaven is my home and earth is not. Help me to live for eternity. Amen.

REFLECT & RESPOND: How does remembering that heaven is your home shift your perspective today? How can you live as a citizen of heaven right now?

DAY 52

Trust His Guarding Peace

"Then you will experience God's peace, which exceeds anything we can understand. His peace will guard your hearts and minds as you live in Christ Jesus."

Philippians 4:7 NLT

Do life's worries ever creep in like uninvited guests?

Our thoughts race, fears intensify, and what-ifs magnify, leading us to quickly feel overwhelmed and overloaded. Thankfully, God offers another option: His peace.

This peace is the presence of Jesus, even in the midst of problems. Paul says it guards your heart and mind. His peace pushes back fear, shields you from anxiety, and quiets the noise of worry.

What's remarkable is that this peace doesn't always make sense. It often comes in situations where peace feels impossible—during uncertainty, in waiting, or in a trial. Yet, it holds you secure, reminding you that God is in control and you are safe in Him.

Be assured, His peace is actively protecting your heart and mind today. Simply bring everything to Him in prayer, and then trust the safeguard of His peace to stand watch over you.

SPEAK LIFE: "God's peace protects my heart and mind today."

TALK TO GOD: Lord, thank You for Your peace that guards my heart and mind. Remind me to bring everything to You today. Amen.

REFLECT & RESPOND: What worry or fear can you hand over to God today? How will you trust His peace to guard you?

DAY 53

Choose His Will, Not Yours

"Father, if you are willing, please take this cup of suffering away from me. Yet I want your will to be done, not mine."

Luke 22:42 NLT

How have you surrendered to God's will recently?

In the Garden of Gethsemane, Jesus modeled for us how true surrender looks. Even though He was fully God, He chose to submit His will to His Father's, knowing the suffering that was ahead for Him. His prayer wasn't a demand or plea to avoid the cross; instead, it was a humble yielding of *Your will, not Mine.*

Surrender isn't something negative; it's a beautiful act of trusting God. Jesus teaches us that surrender means laying down our desires, fears, and plans to embrace God's perfect purpose for our lives. When you feel overwhelmed by choices, struggles, or uncertainty, surrender is an invitation to find peace and strength, even in the biggest storms.

Don't worry about not having it all figured out. Just do what Jesus did. Simply say, "Your will, not mine, Lord." You'll find His peace in the process, and you'll experience His strength carrying you through every situation.

SPEAK LIFE: "I desire God's will today, not mine."

TALK TO GOD: God, prompt me to surrender everything to You—my desires, fears, plans, life. Amen.

REFLECT & RESPOND: What is most difficult to surrender currently? How can you follow Jesus' example today?

DAY 54

Guard Your Heart

"Guard your heart above all else, for it determines the course of your life."

Proverbs 4:23 NLT

What's been filling your heart lately?

What we allow into our minds and hearts directly impacts how we think, feel, and live. Just as we wouldn't drink water from a muddy stream, it's wise not to let unhealthy or ungodly influences into our lives. The movies we watch, the music and podcasts in which we listen, the books we read, the social media we scroll—all of it feeds something in us.

The enemy is ever so subtle. He won't always tempt us with something obviously destructive; sometimes it's just a steady drip of ideas, values, and images that slowly pull us away from God's truth.

Proverbs 4 is a timely reminder to guard your heart diligently because everything—your words, actions, decisions, and relationships—flows from it. Your heart is worth protecting. God has entrusted it to you to keep it aligned with His, so it overflows with His abundance.

SPEAK LIFE: "I guard my mind and heart by filling them with God's life-giving truth."

TALK TO GOD: Lord, prompt me to examine what I consume. Help me honor You and guard my heart. Amen.

REFLECT & RESPOND: What's something you regularly take in that doesn't align with God's truth? How can you replace it with something that draws you closer to Him?

DAY 55

Reflect

Take a few moments to revisit the days you've just walked. There's no rush here—just honesty and grace. Feel free to journal your answers.

Reflection Prompts:

- ✓ What truth stood out to me this week?
- ✓ Where did I notice God inviting me to stop settling?
- ✓ What challenged me? What encouraged me?
- ✓ What thought/encouragement/hope do I want to carry with me into the coming days?

DAY 56

Rest

Today is a day to rest—not to catch up, fix something, or prove anything. Abundant life includes stopping long enough to receive what God is already offering you.

Sit quietly with God for a few minutes.

Breathe deeply.

Allow any Scripture from the past few days to encourage you.

Let yourself be loved and cared for by your Creator.

DAY 57

Look at God's Masterpiece

"For we are God's masterpiece. He has created us anew in Christ Jesus, so we can do the good things he planned for us long ago."

Ephesians 2:10 NLT

When you look in the mirror, what do you see?

Too often, we notice flaws before beauty. We see what's wrong, not what's wonderful. But God sees something entirely different. He sees a masterpiece.

He designed every detail of you with care: your appearance, your laugh, your talents, even your emotions. Your strengths, sensitivities, and temperament are intentional gifts from Him.

In Jesus, God created you brand new to do the good works He planned a long time ago. You are a one-of-a-kind work of art with a one-of-a-kind purpose. Each day holds opportunities to live out His unique design for your life—to reflect His love, shine His light, and bless others in ways only you can.

Look again. Not through the eyes of the world, but look through your Creator's. You are His masterpiece—loved, intentional, purposeful. Walk boldly into the good works He's prepared for you to do today.

SPEAK LIFE: "I am God's masterpiece, created for good works."

TALK TO GOD: Lord, prompt me to believe I am Your masterpiece. Help me do the good things You have for me. Amen.

REFLECT & RESPOND: Look in the mirror today. Ask God to help you see yourself the way He does.

DAY 58

Lose the Lying Labels

"But the voice spoke again: 'Do not call something unclean if God has made it clean.'"

Acts 10:15 NLT

What labels have you been wearing? Uninvited? Unimportant? A failure?

Labels such as uninvited, unimportant, or a failure are not God's words about you. These kinds of false labels can't stick when God has already spoken truth over you.

Still, we wear these kinds of labels like name tags, often unaware we're doing it. Similar to Peter in Acts 10, God is asking you to see with His eyes. He's asking you to accept how He sees you. What He has made clean, no one can call unclean—not even you.

Ask yourself, *Does God say this about me?* If He doesn't, it's time to peel off the label and toss it in the trash. God has spoken new names over you. Clean. Loved. Redeemed. His.

Today is the day to release false labels and replace them with God's. No more wearing lies. No more living under names that don't belong to you. Walk forward in the freedom of who you truly are in Him.

SPEAK LIFE: "My labels are what God says about me."

TALK TO GOD: God, prompt me to remove the lying labels and to boldly live in Your identity for me. Amen.

REFLECT & RESPOND: What label are you wearing that isn't God's truth? What would it look like to surrender it today?

DAY 59

Be Reminded: He Is Not Far Off

"'His purpose was for the nations to seek after God and perhaps feel their way toward him and find him—though he is not far from any one of us ...'"

Acts 17:27 NLT

Does God feel far away?

Maybe you wonder if He sees the path you are walking. Or you question if He hears you. The truth is this: God is not far off. He never has been—and never will be.

This verse reaffirms that even when you can't sense His presence, or when you feel forgotten or unsure of the way forward, God is near. He's not far from any of His daughters—including you. He's with you. Not just when you're at your best, but especially when you feel lost, weary, unseen, or unsure.

You don't have to go searching far and wide to find Him. He's already in the room. In the quiet. In your questions. In your next breath. He simply invites you to reach out, to seek Him, to know that He is right here.

SPEAK LIFE: "Even when He feels far away, God is with me."

TALK TO GOD: God, guide me to trust You are here, even when I can't feel Your presence."

REFLECT & RESPOND: How would your day change if you lived remembering that God is near—even now? Whisper a prayer of trust today and rest in His presence.

DAY 60

Rejoice in Today

*"This is the day the Lord has made.
We will rejoice and be glad in it."*

Psalm 118:24 NLT

Do we treat each day as the amazing gift it is?

Each one God gives us is unique, filled with purpose, and worthy of appreciation and celebration. We can easily focus on the next thing or get pulled back to the past. However, God calls us to rejoice right here, right now—and to embrace the moment we're in with joy and gladness.

When we choose joy in the present, we're not ignoring challenges or pretending everything's perfect. Rather, we're recognizing that God is with us in every second, every breath. We remember He has made this day and this moment with His goodness and grace. When our lives are filtered through joy, even ordinary moments are filled with hope.

Today, live in the joy of the present. Let go of rushing ahead or looking backward. Celebrate this day as God's gift, and experience His peace, purpose, and presence in every moment.

SPEAK LIFE: "I rejoice in this day and celebrate God's presence."

TALK TO GOD: God, thank You for making today. Help me to rejoice and be glad in it and in every day forward. Amen.

REFLECT & RESPOND: What distractions keep you from fully embracing today? How can you live with joy in the present moment?

DAY 61

Overflow with Thanks

"So then, just as you received Christ Jesus as Lord, continue to live your lives in him, rooted and built up in him, strengthened in the faith as you were taught, and overflowing with thankfulness."

Colossians 2:6-7 NIV

When was the last time you were so filled with gratitude that it spilled out of you?

A heart that's full of thanks can't help but spill over. Here, Paul depicts a life so established in Jesus—so strengthened by His truth—that thankfulness naturally overflows. It's an abundant, contagious expression of joy in the One Who provides everything.

When we remember who we are in Jesus, what He's done for us, and the hope we have in Him, thanksgiving is our natural response. Gratitude lifts our eyes from what we don't have and fixes them on what we do. As we live this way, others notice. Our overflowing thanks can encourage others to see God's goodness for themselves.

Allow your gratitude to spill over—into your words, actions, prayers, and presence. You may never know whose heart it will impact.

SPEAK LIFE: "My thanks overflows to bless God and others."

TALK TO GOD: Lord, help me to spill out with thanks so others can see You through me. Amen.

REFLECT & RESPOND: Where has God been especially faithful in your life this week? How can you express thanks in a way that encourages someone else today?

DAY 62

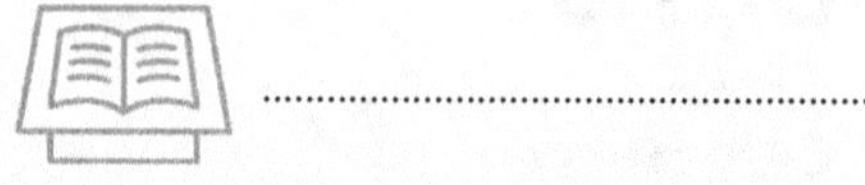

Reflect

Take a few moments to revisit the days you've just walked. There's no rush here—just honesty and grace. Feel free to journal your answers.

Reflection Prompts:

- ✓ What truth stood out to me this week?
- ✓ Where did I notice God inviting me to stop settling?
- ✓ What challenged me? What encouraged me?
- ✓ What thought/encouragement/hope do I want to carry with me into the coming days?

DAY 63

Rest

Today is a day to rest—not to catch up, fix something, or prove anything. Abundant life includes stopping long enough to receive what God is already offering you.

Sit quietly with God for a few minutes.

Breathe deeply.

Allow any Scripture from the past few days to encourage you.

Let yourself be loved and cared for by your Creator.

DAY 64

Receive God's Rest

"It is useless for you to work so hard from early morning until late at night, anxiously working for food to eat; for God gives rest to his loved ones."

Psalm 127:2 NLT

Do you ever feel like your value is tied to how much you accomplish?

Somewhere along the way, many of us began to believe that what we produce determines our worth. We measure our days—and sometimes ourselves—by how much we get done. Yet, we are not machines built for constant output. We are beloved daughters of God, created with limits and the need for rest.

Solomon reminds us that running ourselves ragged is not God's best. He gives rest as a gift—not as a reward for effort; but instead, rest is a provision of His grace. Rest is not laziness; it's living according to the truth that we are more than what we produce.

Pause today. Breathe deeply. Let this truth sink in: you are deeply loved even when you're not "getting things done." God delights in you as His daughter, not in your to-do list.

SPEAK LIFE: "God loves me more than my to-do list."

TALK TO GOD: God, guide me to remember that my to-do list doesn't define me. You do. Amen.

REFLECT & RESPOND: Where in your life have you been running like a machine? What is one way you can receive God's gift of rest today?

DAY 65

Align Before You Assign

"Commit to the Lord whatever you do, and he will establish your plans."

Proverbs 16:3 NIV

How do you begin tasks—on your own, or do you involve God?

In a world that recognizes efficiency—make lists, assign tasks, keep moving—Solomon encourages us in another direction. He guides us to not act first; instead, align with God. Before we assign steps, set goals, or fill our calendars, it's wise to first commit it all to God.

Aligning with God is what we do to ensure fruitfulness. When our work begins in prayerful surrender, our tasks become more than checkboxes; they become opportunities to partner with and serve God. Instead of striving on our own to achieve success, we trust God to establish what matters most: His plans and purposes.

What would it look like for you to pause today before assigning tasks or making plans? Could you take a moment to invite God into your calendar, your responsibilities, and even your to-do list? This small shift turns ordinary planning into intentional partnering with Him.

SPEAK LIFE: "I pause to align myself with God before moving forward."

TALK TO GOD: God, align my heart, plans, will, and assignments with Yours. Guide me to seek You first before taking action. Amen.

REFLECT & RESPOND: Where do you tend to rush ahead with assignments before seeking alignment? Take five quiet minutes today to commit your tasks to the Lord, one by one.

DAY 66

Stop Wanting What She Has

"For wherever there is jealousy and selfish ambition, there you will find disorder and evil of every kind."

James 3:16 NLT

Do you ever wish you had what she has?

Her home looks nicer, her life looks easier, her blessings appear bigger. This kind of comparison never leads us to peace and satisfaction, only to jealousy and discontent. James makes it clear how comparison creates chaos and wickedness—not a full life.

If you're struggling with comparison today, remember God's provision for you is never second-best. He doesn't give you the leftovers. What He's given you today is what He knows you need for this season. You don't have to yearn for what someone else has or feel behind because your journey looks different. Her blessings were designed for her; yours were chosen specifically for you.

You don't need what she has. God has given you a Shepherd who provides, a Father who sees, and a Savior who laid down everything so you can live free. What could possibly compare to that?

SPEAK LIFE: "God provides all I need; I don't need what others have."

TALK TO GOD: God, when I want what others have, switch my focus to what You've already provided for me. Amen.

REFLECT & RESPOND: Where in life are you tempted to compare? How can you shift your focus to what God has already given you?

DAY 67

Notice Needs and Respond

"But Peter said, 'I don't have any silver or gold for you. But I'll give you what I have. In the name of Jesus Christ the Nazarene, get up and walk!'"

Acts 3:6 NLT

When you hear the word generosity, does money often come to mind?

Peter shows us that generosity includes much more than finances. He didn't have coins to give the man begging at the temple gate. Instead, he offered something far more valuable: the power of Jesus. That moment not only changed the man's mobility, but it changed his life forever.

God's generosity through you impacts others, too. Maybe it's offering encouragement when someone feels discouraged, listening to a friend who needs to talk, sharing your skills to bless another, or praying when someone needs hope. Sometimes the most generous gift isn't from your wallet at all. It's from your heart.

True generosity is simply noticing needs and responding with what you have. This kind of giving can multiply blessings beyond what money alone can accomplish.

SPEAK LIFE: "God calls me to be generous, not just with money."

TALK TO GOD: God, open my eyes to see the needs of those around me, and prompt me to give to others as You instruct. Amen.

REFLECT & RESPOND: When were you impacted by someone who blessed you with something other than money? What non-financial gift could you offer this week to someone else?

DAY 68

Invite God into the Details

"The Lord directs the steps of the godly. He delights in every detail of their lives."

Psalm 37:23 NLT

Do you believe God cares about the details of your life?

God isn't only concerned about the big picture; He's present in the details, too. King David reminds us that God is actively involved in it all. Not only in the direction of our lives, but also in the little, seemingly insignificant things. He delights in guiding each step we take, even the ones that feel minuscule or uncertain.

You can't see the full path ahead, but God can. What may feel like a detour or delay to you is a part of His perfect plan. God's role is to control the outcome, and yours is simply to walk faithfully, one step at a time, trusting Him along the way.

Today, invite God into the details. Surrender your plans, and trust Him to direct each step you take.

SPEAK LIFE: "I trust God to guide me in every step today."

TALK TO GOD: Lord, I don't need to control the outcome. I just need to simply take the next step with You. Remind me of this when I forget. Amen.

REFLECT & RESPOND: What first step is God asking you to take right now? How does it encourage you to know He delights in every detail of your life?

DAY 69

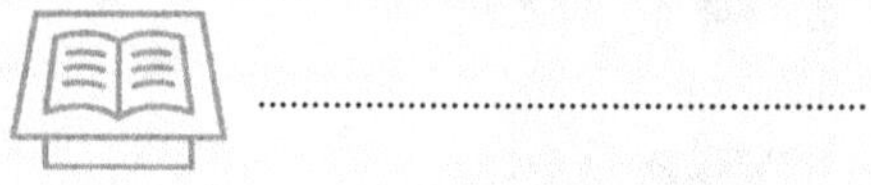

Reflect

Take a few moments to revisit the days you've just walked. There's no rush here—just honesty and grace. Feel free to journal your answers.

Reflection Prompts:

- ✓ What truth stood out to me this week?
- ✓ Where did I notice God inviting me to stop settling?
- ✓ What challenged me? What encouraged me?
- ✓ What thought/encouragement/hope do I want to carry with me into the coming days?

DAY 70

Rest

Today is a day to rest—not to catch up, fix something, or prove anything. Abundant life includes stopping long enough to receive what God is already offering you.

Sit quietly with God for a few minutes.

Breathe deeply.

Allow any Scripture from the past few days to encourage you.

Let yourself be loved and cared for by your Creator.

DAY 71

Believe What You Can't See

"Faith shows the reality of what we hope for; it is the evidence of things we cannot see."

Hebrews 11:1 NLT

When was the last time you said, "I'll believe it when I see it"?

We live in a world that continues to proclaim this line of thinking. Faith, however, flips that thinking upside down: *we believe even when we don't yet see it.*

God's reality is often hidden beyond what's visible. His purposes are unfolding, even when we only see the waiting, the wondering, or the impossible. Faith assures us that His promises are already true, even before they appear in our lives.

Think about Noah. He built the ark before the first raindrop fell. Or think about Abraham. He trusted God's promise of descendants before he had children. They weren't walking by what they saw; they were walking by faith in the unseen reality of God.

This same reality is available to you today. When life looks uncertain, remember that God is still working. The unseen is sometimes where God does His most powerful work.

SPEAK LIFE: "When I can't see God at work, I have faith He is."

TALK TO GOD: God, remind me when I can't see progress in my circumstances that You are working behind the scenes. Amen.

REFLECT & RESPOND: What promise from God can you hold onto with faith today? How does knowing God is at work in the unseen give you peace right now?

DAY 72

Follow the Spirit's Leading

"Since we are living by the Spirit, let us follow the Spirit's leading in every part of our lives."

Galatians 5:25 NLT

Do you invite the Holy Spirit into every part of your day?

Walking with God isn't meant to be a Sunday-morning-only stroll. Paul reminds us that if we belong to Jesus and live by the Spirit, we are encouraged to follow His leading in every part of our lives, including the big decisions and small moments.

The Holy Spirit leads us gently, consistently, and wisely. He prompts us to extend grace, to fight off temptation, to live patiently through frustration, and to pray instead of worry. He guides our steps and transforms our hearts—if we're willing to listen and follow His lead.

This kind of daily surrender is beautifully freeing. You no longer need to navigate today in your own strength. The Spirit is your Helper, Guide, and Comforter, ready to lead you one step at a time.

Today, pause and ask the Spirit to lead you, and choose to follow wherever He guides.

SPEAK LIFE: "I invite the Holy Spirit into every part of my day."

TALK TO GOD: God, thank You for the Holy Spirit. I invite His presence into my life. Help me rely on His guidance today. Amen.

REFLECT & RESPOND: When was the last time you felt the Spirit prompting you? How can you intentionally follow His leading today?

DAY 73

Live as His Daughter

"For you are all children of God through faith in Christ Jesus."

Galatians 3:26 NLT

Do you ever feel like just another face in the crowd—overlooked, forgotten, unseen?

You are not just another face to God. God's Word makes it clear: you are His child—His daughter. Not only in name, but more importantly, in relationship.

Your Heavenly Father never withdraws His love, never stops pursuing your heart, and never forgets you. He has good things in store for your life. He sees you, knows you, and invites you to be near Him.

When you're anxious, He holds your hand. When you're unsure, He leads your steps. When you're overwhelmed, He meets your needs. He always provides.

Even when life feels heavy, you can come to Him anytime, confident you're safe and secure in His arms. He's never ashamed of you or disappointed in you. He delights in you—not because of what you do. He delights in you because of who you are—His.

The good news is you don't have to earn His affection. You already have it. You're not just a face in the crowd. You're a daughter of the King.

SPEAK LIFE: "God calls me daughter. I am His."

TALK TO GOD: Lord God, when I doubt, continue to remind me I am Your daughter, loved and secure. Amen.

REFLECT & RESPOND: How has your Heavenly Father shown His love for you recently? Write it down and thank Him for His presence.

DAY 74

Wait Quietly and Trust God

"I wait quietly before God, for my victory comes from him."

Psalm 62:1 NLT

Are you feeling pressure to prove yourself or hold everything together right now?

Psalm 62:1 suggests something different: quiet waiting. Not frantic striving. Not forcing outcomes. Just resting in the truth that victory comes from God alone, not from effort or perfection.

Waiting quietly before God isn't about doing nothing. It's all about trusting Him enough to halt trying to control every detail of your life. It's choosing to believe that God is already at work, even when you don't yet see anything happening. When your heart is quiet before Him, His strength fills you without any sort of striving.

So much of our exhaustion comes from carrying responsibilities God never asked us to shoulder. When we release the need to prove, perform, or rush ahead, however, we open up space for God's power to move on our behalf.

Today, practice quiet trust. Let God fight the battles you can't win on your own. Your victory doesn't depend on you; it comes from Him.

SPEAK LIFE: "God is in control. I trust Him."

TALK TO GOD: Lord God, instead of proving myself or striving on my own, help me to wait quietly and trust You in all circumstances. Amen.

REFLECT & RESPOND: What's one area you are tempted to fix yourself? How is God calling you to quietly trust Him today?

DAY 75

Hear His Invitation

"The Lord says: 'These people come near to me with their mouth and honor me with their lips, but their hearts are far from me. Their worship of me is based on merely human rules they have been taught …'"

Isaiah 29:13 NIV

When was the last time your time with God felt alive instead of routine?

We can easily slip into a pattern: praying because we should, going to church out of habit, or reading Scripture to check it off the list. We go through the motions while our hearts drift farther away. Yet, God gently calls us back from empty routines and forward into a vibrant relationship.

God isn't after your performance. He simply wants your heart.

He desires real connection with you, one that's not dictated by a checklist. He wants time that is sincere, not scripted—time that is prompted by anticipation, not obligation.

There's nothing ritualistic about a real, authentic relationship with God. It's alive. It's growing. It's life-changing.

Today, hear His invitation: *Come to me. Let's walk through this life together.*

SPEAK LIFE: "I draw close to God today out of love, not out of duty."

TALK TO GOD: God, show me how to connect with You in a meaningful and sincere way today. Amen.

REFLECT & RESPOND: Where have routines crept into your relationship with God? What might change if you surrendered your time to Him?

DAY 76

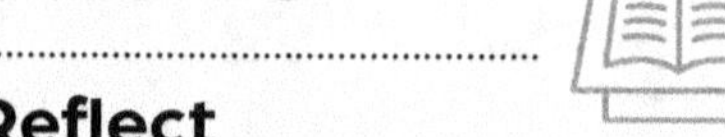

Reflect

Take a few moments to revisit the days you've just walked. There's no rush here—just honesty and grace. Feel free to journal your answers.

Reflection Prompts:

- ✓ What truth stood out to me this week?
- ✓ Where did I notice God inviting me to stop settling?
- ✓ What challenged me? What encouraged me?
- ✓ What thought/encouragement/hope do I want to carry with me into the coming days?

DAY 77

Rest

Today is a day to rest—not to catch up, fix something, or prove anything. Abundant life includes stopping long enough to receive what God is already offering you.

Sit quietly with God for a few minutes.

Breathe deeply.

Allow any Scripture from the past few days to encourage you.

Let yourself be loved and cared for by your Creator.

DAY 78

Follow Without the Map

"The Lord had said to Abram, 'Leave your native country, your relatives, and your father's family, and go to the land that I will show you ...'"

Genesis 12:1 NLT

How has God asked you to release something before revealing what was next?

Abram wasn't given a map or a detailed plan. God simply said, "Leave... and I will show you." The parting came prior to the promise. Before the new chapter began, something familiar had to be left behind.

God works this way with us, too. He invites us to let go of what feels safe—old habits, old fears, or comfortable places that keep us from growing. He asks us to trust Him enough to move forward without first seeing the path ahead.

When God calls you to release something, it's never to leave you empty. It's always the opposite: to make room for what He is preparing.

Today, ask Him what He's inviting you to release, and trust Him to show you the rest in His perfect timing. You can trust Him.

SPEAK LIFE: "God will never mislead me. He knows what He's doing."

TALK TO GOD: God, what are You asking me to let go of today? Please help me trust You more. Amen.

REFLECT & RESPOND: What is God prompting you to release into His care? How might He be preparing you for what's next?

DAY 79

Live Well Today

"He has shown you, O mortal, what is good. And what does the Lord require of you? To act justly and to love mercy and to walk humbly with your God."

Micah 6:8 NIV

What does it mean to live well?

We wait for the next monumental moment, the big break, the "someday" when everything falls into place. Interestingly, Micah brings it back to simple, daily faithfulness: do what is right, love with compassion, and stay humble as you walk with God.

How you live today matters. It's important. Find joy in the memorable mountaintop experiences—but also in the ordinary Tuesday morning conversations, the small acts of kindness no one else sees, or the way you show up for the people in your life.

God isn't asking you to do everything, but He wants you to be faithful in what He's placed in front of you. This is where true life is found—walking humbly with Him, one step at a time.

What if your greatest impact isn't in some distant future, but it's in the way you live this day?

SPEAK LIFE: "How I live life today matters."

TALK TO GOD: Lord, guide me to live today in a way that matters and honors You and blesses others. Amen.

REFLECT & RESPOND: What simple, good thing can you do in line with Micah 6:8? How might you be faithful with where God has you today?

DAY 80

Remember,
God Cares

"For in him we live and move and exist. As some of your own poets have said, 'We are his offspring.'"

Acts 17:28 NLT

How often do you think about how God is involved in every aspect of your life?

Because we can't see God with our physical eyes, we might fall into the belief that He's far off and removed from us and the daily details of our lives.

Paul corrects this myth with truth. God is intimately involved with us. He provides for our physical well-being and is the Source of our very existence. He sustains us in our actions and movements. Our entire being, will, intelligence, and significance all come from God. We are created by Him and for Him, so it's no wonder He's active in our lives.

The next time you feel God is distant, remember this truth: God created you, and He cares about every detail of your life. Every single one.

Turn to Him, invite Him in, and openly share your heart with Him. He'll remind you of His care for you.

SPEAK LIFE: "God cares about every detail of my life."

TALK TO GOD: Lord, guide me to remember the truth that You created me and care about me, more than I know. Amen.

REFLECT & RESPOND: What simple way can you turn to God today? How will you thank Him for caring so intimately about you?

DAY 81

Partner in Building with God

"Unless the Lord builds the house, the builders labor in vain. Unless the Lord watches over the city, the guards stand watch in vain."

Psalm 127:1 NIV

Where are you relying on effort instead of trust right now?

We sometimes carry two common pressures: the pressure to build and the pressure to protect. We work hard to create stability, success, and security, and we stay alert, trying to make sure nothing falls apart. Yet, Scripture reminds us that without God, even our best efforts can leave us exhausted.

God never asked you to build your life alone or to guard it by your own willpower. When He is the builder, your work has purpose. When He is the watchman, your heart can rest. Partnering with the One who sees what you cannot—and protects what matters most—is key to abundant living.

Today, release the need to control it all or hold everything together. Invite the Lord to both build and watch over your life. You are safest and strongest when you trust Him to do what only He can do.

SPEAK LIFE: "I trust God to build and watch over my life."

TALK TO GOD: Lord, help me release my tendency to rely on my own effort and to build with You. Amen.

REFLECT & RESPOND: What's one way you can partner with God to build with Him today? What prevents you from doing this?

DAY 82

Live Smaller to Live Fuller

"Better one handful with tranquility than two handfuls with toil and chasing after the wind."

Ecclesiastes 4:6 NIV

Are you ever consumed with the restless pursuit of more?

This world continually clamors, "Bigger is better. More is success. Happiness comes from accumulation." Yet, God turns that message upside down. Solomon shares God's truth that life isn't found in two handfuls of striving, but rather, in one handful of peace.

What does this mean? It's all about living smaller and releasing what's unnecessary so we can appreciate what truly matters. It's choosing simplicity over chaos, fullness over exhaustion, and presence over performance. It's saying no to endless chasing, so we can say yes to living the abundant life Jesus offers.

This kind of living is countercultural, but when we live smaller, we live in God's fullness. We discover joy in what we already have, rest in the pace He sets, and space to notice His daily gifts. That's a life far richer than anything "more" can promise.

SPEAK LIFE: "Living smaller with Jesus is a life of abundance."

TALK TO GOD: Lord, when I begin to desire more things from this world, open my eyes to see what You've already given me. Amen.

REFLECT & RESPOND: Where is God inviting you to release the desire for more? What might living smaller look like in your home, schedule, or heart this week?

DAY 83

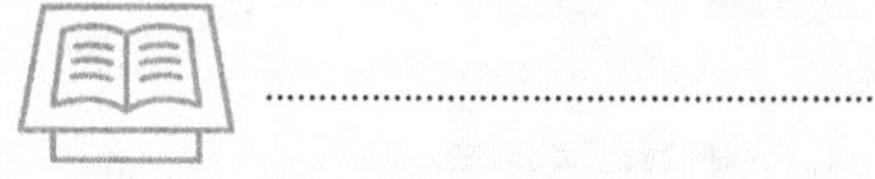

Reflect

Take a few moments to revisit the days you've just walked. There's no rush here—just honesty and grace. Feel free to journal your answers.

Reflection Prompts:

- ✓ What truth stood out to me this week?
- ✓ Where did I notice God inviting me to stop settling?
- ✓ What challenged me? What encouraged me?
- ✓ What thought/encouragement/hope do I want to carry with me into the coming days?

DAY 84

Rest

Today is a day to rest—not to catch up, fix something, or prove anything. Abundant life includes stopping long enough to receive what God is already offering you.

Sit quietly with God for a few minutes.

Breathe deeply.

Allow any Scripture from the past few days to encourage you.

Let yourself be loved and cared for by your Creator.

DAY 85

Give Out
of Love

"If someone has enough money to live well and sees a brother or sister in need but shows no compassion—how can God's love be in that person?"

1 John 3:17 NLT

When was the last time you saw someone in need—and acted?

John's words are convicting and clarifying. Genuine love responds when faced with a need. If we have the resources to help another, but instead close our hearts, John questions whether God's love is truly at work within us. Godly love involves action.

God modeled this perfectly. Out of His immense love, He gave His Son for us (John 3:16). In this same love, He moves us to respond—not out of guilt or pressure; but instead, we respond because God's love always gives.

This giving may be financial support, a warm meal, a listening ear, an offering of encouragement, or faithful prayer. No matter how it looks, this giving always points back to Jesus.

When God's love fills your heart, you can't help but act when you see a need. Allow God's love to move you to compassion today, and watch what Jesus will do through you.

SPEAK LIFE: "God's love flows through me to give to others."

TALK TO GOD: Lord, help me see the needs of others and give out of Your love today. Amen.

REFLECT & RESPOND: When was the last time love moved you to give? What's one way you can give out of love today?

DAY 86

Follow First, Understand Later

"It was by faith that Abraham obeyed when God called him to leave home and go to another land that God would give him as his inheritance. He went without knowing where he was going."

Hebrews 11:8 NLT

Are you waiting to know more before obeying God?

Think about this: Abraham didn't have the details, destination, or timeline. All he had was God's command to go. So, he went. That's faith—choosing to follow first and understand later.

Don't we often want God to explain the details before we move? Courageous obedience trusts God's faithfulness more than our own understanding. Faith says, "If God is leading, I'll follow, even if I don't see the full picture."

If Abraham had waited until everything made sense, he would have missed out on God's planned inheritance. The same is true for us. Our greatest growth often comes—not in knowing the outcomes. Instead, it comes in trusting the One Who does.

You don't have to see the whole road ahead to take the next step. Be like Abraham and trust the One leading you.

SPEAK LIFE: "Even in the unknowns, I trust God."

TALK TO GOD: Lord, remind me I don't need to know the full plan. I just need to trust You. Amen.

REFLECT & RESPOND: Where are you waiting to know more before obeying? What step could you take today, trusting God with the unknowns?

DAY 87

Remember the Fleetingness of Life

"They are like a breath; their days are like a fleeting shadow."

Psalm 144:4 NIV

Does it feel like your life is slipping past you?

David reminds us of the brevity of human life. Like a breath on a cold morning or a shadow that shifts with the sun, our days slip past us quickly, often faster than we realize.

This verse isn't meant to create fear or urgency; it's intended to create awareness. When we remember how fleeting life is, we're motivated to live differently. We concern ourselves less with what doesn't matter and become more intentional with what does. Loving God and loving others matter. Living faithfully matters. Spending time with God matters. How we live each day truly does matter.

God doesn't remind us of the conciseness of life to overwhelm us, but He desires for us to live wisely with Him. Each day is a gift, not a guarantee.

Today, pause and take inventory of what truly matters. Let the shortness of life draw you closer to God and shape how you live and love right now.

SPEAK LIFE: "My life is short, so I live every day as a gift."

TALK TO GOD: Lord God, thank You for reminding me of life's brevity. Help me to live each day wisely with You. Amen.

REFLECT & RESPOND: How are you making what truly matters your priority today? What's one thing God is leading you to adjust?

DAY 88

Rest in His Provision

"Give us today our daily bread."

Matthew 6:11 NIV

Could you use a reminder today of God's perfect provision?

Interestingly, Jesus taught us to pray, not for a week's worth of bread—not even tomorrow's share—but instead, only for today's portion. This brief request is a picture of trusting God as our Provider. Just as He fed Israel with fresh manna in the wilderness, He nourishes us day by day with exactly what we need.

Daily bread points not only to food for our bodies, but also to the grace and strength that sustain our souls. We can't live on yesterday's supply of grace any more than we can live on yesterday's bread. God invites us to come back to Him each morning, empty-handed and dependent, ready to receive His fresh provision.

This keeps us close to Him. It draws us away from self-sufficiency and toward a posture of humility and reliance. Instead of hoarding or laboring, we learn to rest in the Father's faithfulness, confident He won't forget us. Today, we can rest in His provision.

SPEAK LIFE: "God provides all I need for today."

TALK TO GOD: Lord God, some days I find myself worrying about what I don't have yet. Prompt me to trust Your perfect provision. Amen.

REFLECT & RESPOND: Where do you need God's provision most right now? How can you release tomorrow's worries and trust Him for today's supply?

DAY 89

Walk Forgiven and Free

"So now there is no condemnation for those who belong to Christ Jesus."

Romans 8:1 NLT

Have you felt the weight of shame pressing on your heart?

It slips in quietly and whispers lies—replaying mistakes, magnifying regrets, remembering harsh words. Shame is the enemy's voice, trying to trap you in a story Jesus has already rewritten.

In Christ, your identity is no longer tied to what you've done or what's been done to you. You are not your past. You are not your failures. Through Paul, God declares your new reality: there is no condemnation. Not some. Not a little. None.

Jesus carried your shame to the cross so you don't have to bear it any longer. That memory you keep revisiting? Grace covers it. That secret you wish you could erase? Forgiveness answers it. The regret that weighs heavily? Jesus removes it. The burden is lifted. Take a breath. You are now free.

Shame is no longer your story. You're not just forgiven, but you can walk boldly in the freedom Jesus gives today.

SPEAK LIFE: "Through Jesus, I'm forgiven and free."

TALK TO GOD: Lord, help me remember that through You I am no longer condemned. You set me free. Amen.

REFLECT & RESPOND: What would it look like if you lived in the forgiveness Jesus has given you? Take a moment to thank Him for this freedom.

DAY 90

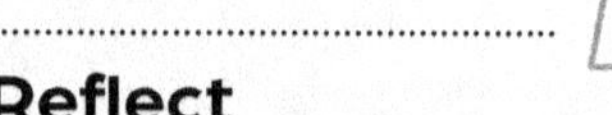
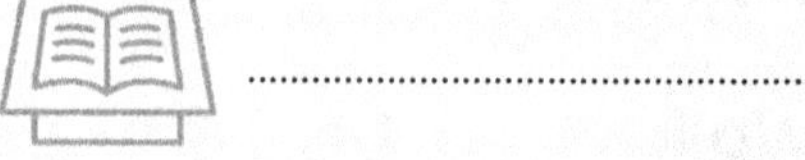

Reflect

Take a few moments to revisit the days you've just walked. There's no rush here—just honesty and grace. Feel free to journal your answers.

Reflection Prompts:

- ✓ What truth stood out to me this week?
- ✓ Where did I notice God inviting me to stop settling?
- ✓ What challenged me? What encouraged me?
- ✓ What thought/encouragement/hope do I want to carry with me into the coming days?

DAY 91

Rest

Today is a day to rest—not to catch up, fix something, or prove anything. Abundant life includes stopping long enough to receive what God is already offering you.

Sit quietly with God for a few minutes.

Breathe deeply.

Allow any Scripture from the past few days to encourage you.

Let yourself be loved and cared for by your Creator.

DAY 92

Accept Your Humanity

"The Lord is like a father to his children, tender and compassionate to those who fear him. For he knows how weak we are; he remembers we are only dust."

Psalm 103:13-14 NLT

Do you ever feel frustrated with your humanity—your limits, emotions, or weaknesses?

God isn't surprised by your frailty. He isn't impatient with your limits or annoyed by your struggles. He knows exactly how you're wired because He formed you, Himself.

David says that God meets us, not with disappointment, but rather with tenderness and compassion. He doesn't expect perfection or strength we don't have. He simply invites us to come as we are, rely on Him, and receive His mercy for today.

Your weaknesses don't frustrate God; they invite His compassion. His heart is never cold toward you. His love isn't dependent on you. His patience doesn't fail when you stumble or fall short.

Take a breath today. Let go of the pressure to be perfect. You are deeply loved by the God who knows you and meets you with gentle mercy, right where you are.

SPEAK LIFE: "God is tender and compassionate to me."

TALK TO GOD: Lord, help me remember that You love me, no matter what. You are never frustrated with my humanity. Amen.

REFLECT & RESPOND: How have you been frustrated with yourself recently? How does it encourage you to remember God isn't frustrated with you?

DAY 93

Wait Dependently and Patiently

"The Lord is good to those who depend on him, to those who search for him."

Lamentations 3:25 NLT

When has waiting felt difficult?

You're ready to move forward, but God's answer is "not yet." This can be discouraging and frustrating—and may challenge you in your walk with God. A truth to remember in times like this: waiting with Him is never wasted.

Lamentations 3 reminds us that God is good to those who depend on Him, to those who search for Him. We may think waiting is passive, but it's not. It's an active choice to trust God's timing and seek Him in the process. While we wait, He molds our hearts, strengthens our faith, and often prepares us for what's ahead in ways we cannot yet see.

The waiting season might feel slow, yes, but it's certainly not stagnant. God is moving behind the scenes, and His plan will be worth your patience. You can rest today knowing His timing is always perfect, even if yours feels delayed.

SPEAK LIFE: "My waiting is not wasted, as God's timing is perfect."

TALK TO GOD: Heavenly Father, remind me today that if You're calling me to wait, Your plan is unfolding perfectly. Amen.

REFLECT & RESPOND: Where in your life is God asking you to wait? How can you use this time to deepen your dependence on Him?

DAY 94

Abide and You'll Thrive

"But they delight in the law of the Lord, meditating on it day and night. They are like trees planted along the riverbank, bearing fruit each season. Their leaves never wither, and they prosper in all they do."

Psalm 1:2-3 NLT

Ever feel like you're merely surviving?

The truth is, you weren't created to just get by—you were made to thrive.

Psalm 1 paints a vivid picture of what happens when life is established in God and His Word. You become like a well-watered tree—secure, nourished, and fruitful in every season. No matter what comes your way, you remain strong as you immerse yourself in His truth.

Thriving comes from abiding and remaining close to God. As you stay connected to Him, fruit appears: love, joy, peace, and patience. Not because of you; it's because His abundant life flows through you.

Abiding isn't something to check off your list or a Sunday-only habit. It's daily trust, returning again and again, sinking your roots deep in His truth. This is where flourishing begins. Abide in Him today, and you'll naturally thrive.

SPEAK LIFE: "I thrive by staying rooted in God and His Word."

TALK TO GOD: Lord, as I abide in You, enable me to thrive in every season. Amen.

REFLECT & RESPOND: What helps you remain connected to God? What's one shift you could make to abide more intentionally this week?

DAY 95

Give Thanks as God's Will

"Be thankful in all circumstances, for this is God's will for you who belong to Christ Jesus."

1 Thessalonians 5:18 NLT

Have you ever wondered what God's will is for your life?

Paul offers a clear answer here: thankfulness. This thankfulness isn't simply a suggestion or a polite gesture. It's God's will for everyone who belongs to Him through Jesus. Why? Because gratitude aligns us with Him. It shifts our focus from what's lacking to His faithful provision. It reminds us of His goodness, even in difficult seasons. Thankfulness is God's best for us.

It doesn't deny what's real, but it offers us God's perspective on His reality. While our circumstances may not change, gratitude changes us: our attitude, our trust, and our joy.

When you choose thankfulness, you're doing more than changing your perspective—you're stepping right into God's will for your life. Gratitude becomes an act of trust and obedience, reminding you that His goodness is present in every circumstance. Today, embrace thankfulness as God's will, and let it shape the way you live.

SPEAK LIFE: "I choose to live out God's will of thankfulness today."

TALK TO GOD: Lord, please guide me to be grateful in every part of today and in the days to come. Amen.

REFLECT & RESPOND: Write down three things you're thankful for today. How does focusing on gratitude change your perspective right now?

DAY 96

Live in Balance

"It's not good to eat too much honey, and it's not good to seek honors for yourself."

Proverbs 25:27 NLT

When recently have you felt out of balance with food or striving?

Food is meant to be a gift from God—fuel for the body He created for you. In our culture, though, eating can quickly become tainted with shame, comparison, or punishment. We label foods as "good" or "bad," measure our worth by a number on a scale, and sometimes use restriction or overindulgence to cope with stress or emotions.

Scripture reminds us of the value of balance. Just as too much honey isn't wise, neither is depriving ourselves in ways that harm our health. Also, just as we can overindulge with food, we can also crave recognition and approval in ways that leave us empty. Both hunger and honor can become unhealthy when we put them first.

God designed food to nourish, strengthen, and sustain us, and He alone is the One who defines our worth. When we treat food and achievement as an act of stewardship, we can make choices that honor our bodies and our hearts—and the God Who made them.

SPEAK LIFE: "God defines my worth, not food or approval."

TALK TO GOD: Heavenly Father, prompt me to live in Your balance in every area of life. Amen.

REFLECT & RESPOND: How do your current habits reflect balance and gratitude? How can you adjust them in the days to come?

DAY 97

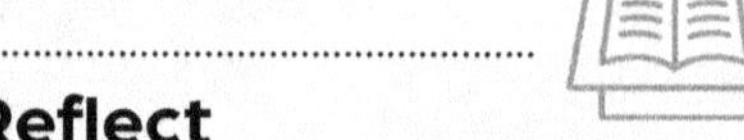

Reflect

Take a few moments to revisit the days you've just walked. There's no rush here—just honesty and grace. Feel free to journal your answers.

Reflection Prompts:

- ✓ What truth stood out to me this week?
- ✓ Where did I notice God inviting me to stop settling?
- ✓ What challenged me? What encouraged me?
- ✓ What thought/encouragement/hope do I want to carry with me into the coming days?

DAY 98

Rest

Today is a day to rest—not to catch up, fix something, or prove anything. Abundant life includes stopping long enough to receive what God is already offering you.

Sit quietly with God for a few minutes.

Breathe deeply.

Allow any Scripture from the past few days to encourage you.

Let yourself be loved and cared for by your Creator.

DAY 99

Share What God Has Done

How often do you tell of God's redeeming work in your life?

We know what God has done in our lives, but do others? David calls us to declare the truth of God's redemption and His saving work in our lives. When we tell others of this truth, we're not only reminding ourselves of God's faithfulness, we're also testifying to others who need to hear it, too.

"Look what God has done in my life!" This declaration isn't bragging; it's equipping others to realize if God did it for you, He can do it for them. Not only this, but God gets all of the glory.

The more you share what God has done, the stronger your faith grows. Then, your witness encourages others to believe it for themselves. You don't need a big stage or perfect circumstances to share your story. Someone you encounter today is a perfect person to tell.

SPEAK LIFE: "God's redeeming power is worth sharing."

TALK TO GOD: Lord, today, equip me to declare what You've done in my life and share it with others. Amen.

REFLECT & RESPOND: When do you typically shy away from sharing what God has done in your life? Who could you share your story with today?

DAY 100

Live in His Gift of Peace

"'I am leaving you with a gift—peace of mind and heart. And the peace I give is a gift the world cannot give. So don't be troubled or afraid …'"

John 14:27 NLT

How often do you pause to remember the gift of peace Jesus has already given you?

Before His departure, Jesus promised His followers something remarkable: His own peace. Not a temporary calm the world offers, but it's a steady, lasting peace that sustains us no matter how life's circumstances swirl around us. This peace is a gift—freely given, not earned or created by us. We simply receive it.

When fear, anxiety, or distraction try to consume us, we can quickly forget this peace is already ours. Jesus' words remind us to rest in His loving provision and to allow His peace to guard our hearts and steady our minds.

His peace is present, available, and strong enough to hold you today. Simply live in it, and while you're at it, thank Jesus for it.

SPEAK LIFE: "I live in the peace of Jesus today."

TALK TO GOD: Jesus, thank You for the gift of Your peace. Help me to live in it today and share it with others. Amen.

REFLECT & RESPOND: Where are life's circumstances causing fear or anxiety? How can you live in the peace Jesus has given you instead?

DAY 101

Keep a Sacred Schedule

"Work willingly at whatever you do, as though you were working for the Lord rather than for people. Remember that the Lord will give you an inheritance as your reward, and that the Master you are serving is Christ."

Colossians 3:23-34 NLT

When was the last time you planned your day with God in mind?

Tasks that demand our attention tend to fill our days, but do they carry eternal value? Our calendars can reflect our activity, but they could also be a map for divine impact. When we plan with God in mind, we stop treating our calendars like checklists and start aligning our schedules with His purposes.

This is when your calendar becomes a sacred schedule. Prioritize your energy, moments, and commitments so your daily rhythm honors God. Ask yourself: *Does this serve me, or does it serve the Lord?*

Your days can be intentional, ordered, and full of purpose. By staying mindful of God's priorities, you create space for what truly matters—prayer, rest, relationships, and sacred moments that last.

SPEAK LIFE: "My schedule reflects God's purposes."

TALK TO GOD: God, show me how to keep a sacred schedule with You in mind. Amen.

REFLECT & RESPOND: Look at your upcoming week and identify where your current plans reflect more activity than purpose. Ask God to help you reorder that space.

DAY 102

Give What's Best

Do you tend to give what's convenient or what's best?

Proverbs reminds us God is honored when we give Him what's best, not what's convenient. Giving the best part of what we produce is an act of trust. It says, "God, You are my Provider. I trust You with everything."

We often give God our leftovers: whatever time, energy, or resources remain after we've cared for ourselves. Yet, honoring Him with the first and best declares that He comes before anything else. Whether it's the first portion of our income, the most focused part of our day, or the creative use of our talents, God delights when we trust Him enough to give freely—and to give to Him first.

Here's the promise: when you put Him first, He takes care of the rest. You can trust God as you give generously today.

SPEAK LIFE: "I honor God with my first and my best."

TALK TO GOD: Lord, You call me to give my best and first, so please equip me to do this daily. Amen.

REFLECT & RESPOND: Where might you be giving God your leftovers instead of your best? What could it look like to offer Him the first part of everything?

DAY 103

Pause in Reverence

"'Can you solve the mysteries of God? Can you discover everything about the Almighty? Such knowledge is higher than the heavens—and who are you? It is deeper than the underworld—what do you know? It is broader than the earth and wider than the sea ...'"

Job 11:7-9 NLT

When was the last time you simply paused to stand in awe of God?

We often approach faith like a puzzle to solve, desiring quick answers and tidy explanations. But God isn't a mystery to master. He's a Person to worship. Job's friend, Zophar, reminds us of the greatness of God. His knowledge extends beyond the heavens, reaches deeper than we can imagine, and stretches wider than the sea.

This truth isn't meant to frustrate us; it's meant to draw us to worship. This kind of awe shifts our perspective. It moves us from striving to surrender, from demanding answers to delighting in Him.

Today, pause in reverence. Worship Him not for what you understand, but rather for Who He's shown Himself to be.

SPEAK LIFE: "God's greatness is worth worshipping today."

TALK TO GOD: God, I stand in awe of You today. I praise You for who You are, and I thank You for Your continued faithfulness in my life. Amen.

REFLECT & RESPOND: What puts you in awe of God the most? Sit with Him today, and worship Him with wonder and praise.

DAY 104

Reflect

Take a few moments to revisit the days you've just walked. There's no rush here—just honesty and grace. Feel free to journal your answers.

Reflection Prompts:

- ✓ What truth stood out to me this week?
- ✓ Where did I notice God inviting me to stop settling?
- ✓ What challenged me? What encouraged me?
- ✓ What thought/encouragement/hope do I want to carry with me into the coming days?

DAY 105

Rest

Today is a day to rest—not to catch up, fix something, or prove anything. Abundant life includes stopping long enough to receive what God is already offering you.

Sit quietly with God for a few minutes.

Breathe deeply.

Allow any Scripture from the past few days to encourage you.

Let yourself be loved and cared for by your Creator.

DAY 106

Store Treasures Above

"Store your treasures in heaven, where moths and rust cannot destroy, and thieves do not break in and steal. Wherever your treasure is, there the desires of your heart will also be."

Matthew 6:20-21 NLT

Where are you storing your treasures—here on earth or in heaven?

This world urges us to collect more stuff, more money, and more status. Yet, Jesus gently redirects our focus and reminds us how earthly treasures are temporary. They fade, break, or get stolen. Eternal treasures, however, never lose their worth, and they never cease.

When we do the things that matter to God—loving others, giving generously, serving faithfully, sharing the truth of Jesus—we are storing up treasures that last forever. Every unseen prayer, every quiet act of mercy, every sacrifice done in the name of Jesus becomes part of heaven's account.

The question isn't whether we're storing treasures, but it's where we're storing them. Jesus reminds us that our hearts follow our treasures. If our greatest treasures are in heaven, our hearts will be too. Let's store our treasures where it matters most.

SPEAK LIFE: "My treasures are in heaven, and so is my heart."

TALK TO GOD: God, help me to accumulate heavenly treasures— the ones that matter, not earthly ones. Amen.

REFLECT & RESPOND: What treasures have you been storing up lately? What's one way you can invest in heavenly treasures throughout your day?

DAY 107

Walk into Today with Courage

"The Lord is my light and my salvation—whom shall I fear? The Lord is the stronghold of my life—of whom shall I be afraid?"

Psalm 27:1 NIV

Who do you turn to when life feels heavy, uncertain, or overwhelming?

Fear wears many disguises, such as worry, doubt, and hesitation. Each whisper lies: *You're not enough. The future is unknown. You're on your own.* Yet, David counters every lie with truth. The Lord is your Light when darkness closes in, your Salvation when doubts appear, and your Strong Tower when life is heavy.

God's strength is strong and steady. His presence brings clarity where confusion threatens to cloud your view. His protection surrounds you when circumstances feel out of control.

David's confidence didn't come from courage within himself; it came from trust in the God who never fails. Good news: that same confidence is available to you today.

Whatever you face, you do not stand alone. You stand in His strength. So, walk into today with courage. God goes before you, stands beside you, and guards you with His unfailing love.

SPEAK LIFE: "The Lord is my strength and stronghold."

TALK TO GOD: Lord, guide me to walk in Your strength today, and remind me fear has no place where You are present. Amen.

REFLECT & RESPOND: What fear or worry feels heavy for you today? How does Psalm 27:1 shift your perspective, facing it in God's strength?

DAY 108

Remember He Loved You First

"But God showed his great love for us by sending Christ to die for us while we were still sinners."

Romans 5:8 NLT

Have you ever felt you needed to clean up before going to God?

Romans 5:8 states a shocking truth: God loved you at your worst. Before you believed, before you changed, before you even desired Him, Jesus went to the cross for you. His love didn't wait for you to be worthy, willing, or ready.

We might think God begins loving us once we "get it together," but the truth is He loved us before we loved Him. His grace meets us in our mess, and His kindness and mercy lead us to love Him and put our faith in Him.

You don't have to earn His affection or perform for His approval. The cross has already declared your place with God. You were loved then. You are loved now.

Walk in this truth today: you don't have to clean up to go to God. Jesus welcomes you with His open arms.

SPEAK LIFE: "I am loved by God."

TALK TO GOD: Heavenly Father, show me how to live out this truth of Your amazing love, and help me share it with others. Amen.

REFLECT & RESPOND: How have you believed you needed to clean up before coming to God? Replace those lies with the truth of Romans 5:8 today.

DAY 109

Receive God's Forgiveness

"He does not punish us for all our sins; he does not deal harshly with us, as we deserve."

Psalm 103:10 NLT

When was the last time you truly considered God's stunning forgiveness?

It's stunning because we haven't earned it; we can't. Yet, He offers it anyway—graciously and abundantly.

Do you ever struggle to receive it? Maybe you continually replay the past, doubt His grace, or believe you need to make amends for what you did. This psalm is a gracious reminder: God doesn't give us what our sins deserve. Amazingly, His mercy completely covers us and rewrites our stories.

You are forgiven. Fully. Freely. Forever. Read that again.

While He removes your sin, He never removes His love. He relishes and remembers you—the one He created, His redeemed one, and the one in whom He delights.

This truth doesn't minimize the wrong, but it magnifies what He's making right. It leads us to live with awestruck gratitude and soul-impacting repentance.

You can walk forward in His grace today—humbled, healed, and hopeful.

SPEAK LIFE: "I am forgiven by God's grace."

TALK TO GOD: God, help me walk in Your truth today, knowing that You forgive me in Your grace and never forget me. Amen.

REFLECT & RESPOND: Do you believe you're fully forgiven? Ask God for forgiveness, and let Psalm 103 speak to your soul today.

DAY 110

Come with Your Whole Heart

"And since we have a great High Priest who rules over God's house, let us go right into the presence of God with sincere hearts fully trusting him ..."

Hebrews 10:21-22a NLT

It feels good to be invited, doesn't it?

There's something special about knowing you're welcome, the door is open, and your name is written on the invitation.

Through Jesus, the way into God's presence is no longer blocked or reserved for a select few. As Hebrews 10 declares, you are invited into the very presence of God! Thankfully, you don't need to fix yourself, rehearse what to say, or prove you're worthy to attend. He welcomes you in—completely, confidently, and continually.

God is always available and welcoming, waiting with arms open wide, ready to meet you with love and grace. He delights when you accept His invitation and come into His presence.

No matter how long it's been or how undeserving you feel, He desires you with Him. Today, come with your whole heart. He is ready and waiting. You belong in His presence.

SPEAK LIFE: "God wants me with Him. I draw near to Him today."

TALK TO GOD: Lord, help me to come to You with a sincere heart. I desire to be close to you. Amen.

REFLECT & RESPOND: What keeps you from drawing close to God? What's one step you can take toward Him today?

DAY 111

Reflect

Take a few moments to revisit the days you've just walked. There's no rush here—just honesty and grace. Feel free to journal your answers.

Reflection Prompts:

- ✓ What truth stood out to me this week?
- ✓ Where did I notice God inviting me to stop settling?
- ✓ What challenged me? What encouraged me?
- ✓ What thought/encouragement/hope do I want to carry with me into the coming days?

DAY 112

Rest

Today is a day to rest—not to catch up, fix something, or prove anything. Abundant life includes stopping long enough to receive what God is already offering you.

Sit quietly with God for a few minutes.

Breathe deeply.

Allow any Scripture from the past few days to encourage you.

Let yourself be loved and cared for by your Creator.

DAY 113

Keep Laying It Down

"My old self has been crucified with Christ. It is no longer I who live, but Christ lives in me. So I live in this earthly body by trusting in the Son of God, who loved me and gave himself for me."

Galatians 2:20 NLT

What have you surrendered that hasn't stayed that way?

Worries, habits, or fears have a way of creeping back in, don't they? This doesn't mean you've failed; instead, you're human. God isn't impatient with your process or progress; He's present with you in it.

Every time you release something again, you're choosing to trust Him once more. You're saying, "I believe You can handle this better than I." Repeated surrender isn't a weak faith. It's strong. It reminds you that your life is not your own and that His ways are always better.

Don't let the weariness of laying it down again deter you. Don't be embarrassed or discouraged. Think of it this way: each surrender is an act of worship, a reminder of Who is in control. God never tires of meeting you, right where you are.

SPEAK LIFE: "I keep laying down what was never mine to carry."

TALK TO GOD: God, when I continue to surrender the same thing over and over, remind me of Your patience and grace. Amen.

REFLECT & RESPOND: What's one thing you've surrendered more than once? How can you remind yourself of God's grace today?

DAY 114

Dwell on the Good

"And now, dear brothers and sisters, one final thing. Fix your thoughts on what is true, and honorable, and right, and pure, and lovely, and admirable. Think about things that are excellent and worthy of praise."

Philippians 4:8 NLT

Have you ever realized what you think can directly impact your life?

Your thoughts shape your emotions, actions, and even your faith. Apostle Paul invites you to be intentional about what you dwell on—to actively think about what's good and true.

Of course, we experience difficulties in this life, so this isn't about ignoring them or pretending life is perfect. Instead, it involves training yourself to think on truth, beauty, and kindness, even in the not-so-simple moments. When you focus on what's honorable and admirable, you invite God's hope and peace into your life.

Today, choose to filter your thoughts through gratitude and grace. Practice turning away from what's negative, and redirect your attention to the positive. You won't just impact your world; you'll influence the lives of those around you, too.

SPEAK LIFE: "I choose to focus on what's good, true, and worthy of praise."

TALK TO GOD: God, align my thoughts with Yours. Help me see the good today. Amen.

REFLECT & RESPOND: What are three "good things" you notice around you right now? How can changing your focus impact your attitude today?

DAY 115

Take Care of You

"Dear friend, I hope all is well with you and that you are as healthy in body as you are strong in spirit."

3 John 1:2 NLT

Do you ever separate your spiritual life from your physical life?

Your health and your entire being matter to God. He designed every part of your life—physically, mentally, emotionally, and spiritually. He knows the best ways for you to fully thrive. God never meant for parts of you to be at odds. He created them to work together, each affecting the other.

When you care for yourself, you're not being selfish. You're stewarding what God's entrusted to you. When life makes taking care of yourself feel impossible, remember that He sees you. He's not standing over you with a list of demands; He's gently inviting you into a healthier way of living because He loves you. Bottom line: He desires His best for you.

Your health is not about perfection. It's about a beautiful partnership with the One Who made you. Take care of yourself today.

SPEAK LIFE: "I partner with God in taking care of myself."

TALK TO GOD: Lord God, guide me in the ways You desire for me to care for my entire being. Amen.

REFLECT & RESPOND: What can you do today to care for your health? If you're not sure, go to God and ask Him.

DAY 116

Find Strength in His Joy

"Nehemiah said, 'Go and enjoy choice food and sweet drinks, and send some to those who have nothing prepared. This day is holy to our Lord. Do not grieve, for the joy of the Lord is your strength.'"

Nehemiah 8:10 NIV

Life can be draining some days, can't it?

Unexpected interruptions, endless tasks, and the weight of other people's needs can deplete our daily energy. Nehemiah reminds us that our true strength doesn't come from ourselves or others. Instead, it comes from the Lord's joy.

This joy is not the kind we receive from others or from our pleasant circumstances, which is fleeting and changing. This is true joy. It's a divine gift and a powerful inner resource that God provides to His children. It's one that lasts, sustains, and strengthens us in times of trial, equipping, and perseverance.

Receive His joy today. Allow it to strengthen you when the demands of this world weigh heavily. You'll be equipped to serve from a place of fullness, not emptiness—and from joy, not exhaustion.

SPEAK LIFE: "God's joy sustains me, equips me, and allows me to live fully in Him."

TALK TO GOD: Heavenly Father, I receive Your joy today. Strengthen me through it to serve You and others well. Amen.

REFLECT & RESPOND: In what area of life are you feeling depleted or empty? How will you embrace the joy of the Lord in that space?

DAY 117

Rely on Him

Do you ever believe you need more to live a life that pleases God?

Peter reminds us that God has already given us everything we need through His divine power at work in us to live a faithful life. We aren't sufficient because of ourselves, but we become sufficient as we grow in relationship with Him.

This means your life today isn't determined by your own resources, energy, or abilities. It's established in the One Who calls and equips you. His power never depletes. His provision never cuts corners. His timing is always right.

Instead of relying on yourself, pause and rest in this truth: in Jesus, you already have what you need to live faithfully. As you live from that fullness, His abundance naturally flows through you.

SPEAK LIFE: "God has given me everything I need."

TALK TO GOD: God, when I think I need more, help me remember that You've given me what I need to live a godly life. Amen.

REFLECT & RESPOND: Where is God teaching you to rely on His provision? How will you rest in this truth today?

DAY 118

Reflect

Take a few moments to revisit the days you've just walked. There's no rush here—just honesty and grace. Feel free to journal your answers.

Reflection Prompts:

- ✓ What truth stood out to me this week?
- ✓ Where did I notice God inviting me to stop settling?
- ✓ What challenged me? What encouraged me?
- ✓ What thought/encouragement/hope do I want to carry with me into the coming days?

DAY 119

Rest

Today is a day to rest—not to catch up, fix something, or prove anything. Abundant life includes stopping long enough to receive what God is already offering you.

Sit quietly with God for a few minutes.

Breathe deeply.

Allow any Scripture from the past few days to encourage you.

Let yourself be loved and cared for by your Creator.

DAY 120

Don't Wait to Be Ready

"Farmers who wait for perfect weather never plant. If they watch every cloud, they never harvest."

Ecclesiastes 11:4 NLT

Do you ever delay obedience because you're waiting for the "right time"?

We think we'll act, serve, or give when we feel more prepared, when our schedule opens up, or when we have more money. Yet, Scripture warns us: if we wait until the conditions are perfect, we'll never move forward. Life will always give us reasons to hesitate.

It's impossible to have everything figured out before we act, but we can trust God, Who knows it all. The farmer doesn't know which seed will bear fruit, but he plants anyway. Likewise, you may not see immediate results from your giving, serving, or moving forward, but God promises a harvest in His perfect time.

The urgency isn't in rushing; it's in acting in obedient faith. Don't let fear of not being ready keep you from obeying God today. Step forward now, and trust Him with the outcome.

SPEAK LIFE: "I will act in faith today, trusting God with the results."

TALK TO GOD: God, in my hesitancy today, prompt me to move. Help me to be obedient to Your call and trust You with the results. Amen.

REFLECT & RESPOND: What's one act of generosity you've been delaying until the "right time"? How can you take one small step today?

DAY 121

Live Simply Before God

"And now, Israel, what does the Lord your God ask of you but to fear the Lord your God, to walk in obedience to him, to love him, to serve the Lord your God with all your heart and with all your soul ..."

Deuteronomy 10:12 NIV

Do you ever wonder what kind of life God desires for us?

Through Moses, God gave Israel a beautifully clear picture of what He desires: reverence, obedience, love, service, and wholehearted devotion. This isn't a complicated checklist; it's a life fully aligned with Him.

Fearing the Lord means living with awe-filled reverence, trusting His wisdom, and responding with humble obedience. It's choosing to honor Him above everything else, letting His character shape our thoughts, decisions, and actions each day. Out of that reverence, love and service flow naturally. God isn't asking for our perfection; He's inviting us to walk closely with Him in everyday life.

When our hearts are turned toward Him, following God becomes less about performance and more about relationship. This is the simple, wholehearted life He desires.

SPEAK LIFE: "God desires for me to walk closely with Him."

TALK TO GOD: God, I sometimes make my relationship with You too complicated. Help me to remember to simply walk with You daily. Amen.

REFLECT & RESPOND: How have you complicated your relationship with God? Write a short prayer committing your heart and soul to Him today.

DAY 122

Remember the Kingdom Where You Belong

"Since we are receiving a Kingdom that is unshakable, let us be thankful and please God by worshiping him with holy fear and awe."

Hebrews 12:28 NLT

Does the world around you ever feel fragile?

Systems fail, leaders disappoint, and circumstances change quickly. As followers of Jesus, however, we live with security in a kingdom this world can't understand: the kingdom of God. Scripture reminds us this kingdom cannot be shaken. It cannot collapse, decay, or be snatched from us.

This truth steadies us when life feels uncertain or when we see what's temporary begin to crumble. Gratitude becomes our natural response to this unshakable reality. When we lift our hands in praise, we declare we trust the One Who holds everything steady, including us. We know our footing is secure, and our future is unshakable.

If this world feels like it's falling apart around you today, remember the kingdom where you belong. You are safe and secure in His caring hands.

SPEAK LIFE: "Even when this world feels shaky, I am secure in God's kingdom."

TALK TO GOD: Lord, when life appears unsteady, help me remember that Your kingdom is sure and secure. In it, so am I. Amen.

REFLECT & RESPOND: Where in your life are you fearful because of what's shaking around you? How can gratitude shift your focus back to God's unshakable kingdom today?

DAY 123

Rely on the Advocate

"But when the Father sends the Advocate as my representative—that is, the Holy Spirit—he will teach you everything and will remind you of everything I have told you."

John 14:26 NLT

Do you ever feel you're left to figure life out on your own?

The good news: you're not. Jesus promised His disciples that after He returned to the Father, the Holy Spirit would come and dwell within them. That same Holy Spirit resides in all who live for Jesus today.

If that's you, He's already guiding, empowering, and leading you. When you feel uncertain, He gives wisdom. When you can't decide, He provides direction. When lies try to fill your mind, He reminds you of Jesus' truth.

The Holy Spirit is not reserved for just a few moments in life. He is God's constant gift to everyone who believes in Jesus. He is your continual source of courage, clarity, and comfort.

Today, you don't have to figure it out on your own. God's Spirit goes with you, lives in you, and equips you for every moment.

SPEAK LIFE: "The Holy Spirit is always with me, empowering and guiding."

TALK TO GOD: God, prompt me today to rely on the Holy Spirit's leading in every situation. Amen.

REFLECT & RESPOND: Where in your life do you need the Spirit's help right now? How will you pause to listen for His guidance?

DAY 124

Accept His Wholeness

"So you also are complete through your union with Christ, who is the head over every ruler and authority."

Colossians 2:10 NLT

Have you recently felt fragmented or broken?

Some days you may feel anything but whole—crushed by disappointment, failure, or grief. You look at your life and see pieces that don't seem to fit, cracks you can't mend, and gaps you don't know how to fill.

The world tries to convince you that you need to do more, heal faster, or prove yourself before you can be considered whole. God says something else, though: your completeness is already secure in Jesus. Your union with Him means nothing is missing. Every piece is in place, even when it doesn't feel like it.

You no longer have to pretend to have it all together. You don't have to hide the cracks or patch up the pain. You can bring what's broken to the One Who holds all things—including you—together.

Today, allow His wholeness to fill every place that feels empty. You are whole because He is whole.

SPEAK LIFE: "I am complete and whole in Jesus."

TALK TO GOD: Lord, in the places that still feel empty or broken, prompt me to offer them to You. Amen.

REFLECT & RESPOND: Where do you feel incomplete or unworthy? Invite Jesus into that space today, trusting His wholeness to cover you.

DAY 125

Reflect

Take a few moments to revisit the days you've just walked. There's no rush here—just honesty and grace. Feel free to journal your answers.

Reflection Prompts:

- ✓ What truth stood out to me this week?
- ✓ Where did I notice God inviting me to stop settling?
- ✓ What challenged me? What encouraged me?
- ✓ What thought/encouragement/hope do I want to carry with me into the coming days?

DAY 126

Rest

Today is a day to rest—not to catch up, fix something, or prove anything. Abundant life includes stopping long enough to receive what God is already offering you.

Sit quietly with God for a few minutes.

Breathe deeply.

Allow any Scripture from the past few days to encourage you.

Let yourself be loved and cared for by your Creator.

DAY 127

Keep the Conversation Going

"Never stop praying."

1 Thessalonians 5:17 NLT

We can make prayer complicated, can't we?

We might believe we need to pray a certain way, in a special place, at certain times, using spiritual words. Is this God's desire—for it to be so complicated?

We're instructed to pray continually. Simply stated, prayer is conversing with God. It's a back-and-forth, heart-to-heart connection between you and your Creator. Not long, formal, or fancy; instead, it's more like talking to a trusted friend.

Yes, sometimes prayer looks like dedicated "quiet time" with God. Other times, it's a whisper during the meeting, a sigh at the kitchen sink, or a thankful thought as you watch the sunset. Prayer can be the backdrop of life—part of your everyday rhythm.

God rejoices when He hears from you. He loves it when you converse with Him. He is pleased when you draw near to Him. Without expecting perfection or measuring your words, He simply wants you—and time with you.

So, talk to Him today. Often. About everything. Keep the conversation going. He's ready and waiting.

SPEAK LIFE: "Prayer is a natural part of my day."

TALK TO GOD: Lord, prompt me to talk with You about everything throughout my day. May we share an ongoing dialogue. Amen.

REFLECT & RESPOND: When in your day do you most naturally talk to God? How can you simply keep your conversation going?

DAY 128

Be Where Your Feet Are

"'So don't worry about tomorrow, for tomorrow will bring its own worries. Today's trouble is enough for today ...'"

Matthew 6:34 NLT

When was the last time you were fully present?

The world we live in tugs at our attention—to the next deadline, the next goal, the next thing on the list. Jesus, however, invites us into a slower, more stable way: to live fully in each moment.

When we focus on tomorrow's unknowns, we miss the blessings God has for us today. Matthew reminds us not to worry about tomorrow. Worry tries to convince us that focusing on the future will somehow make us prepared; consequently, it only drains us of today's joy and peace.

Being where your feet are is choosing to be where God is in this moment. Pause to breathe deeply, notice His presence, and trust that He'll meet you right here. When you give your full attention to right now, you are able to receive all He has for you. You won't miss a single thing. Don't be anywhere except where your feet are today.

SPEAK LIFE: "I live fully present, receiving all God has for me."

TALK TO GOD: God, guide me to be present with You and others today. Thank you. Amen.

REFLECT & RESPOND: What tends to pull you away from the present moment? How can you intentionally slow down today to notice God's presence?

DAY 129

Embrace His Rhythm of Rest

"On the seventh day God had finished his work of creation, so he rested from all his work. And God blessed the seventh day and declared it holy, because it was the day when he rested from all his work of creation."

Genesis 2:2-3 NLT

When was the last time you truly rested?

Even before sin entered the world, rest was part of God's plan. On the seventh day of creation, God rested, but it was not because He was tired. He set a rhythm for His people. Rest was woven into the very fabric of life, from God's own example.

When you pause, you acknowledge the world doesn't revolve around your constant activity. Rest is a reminder that God is in control and that you are more than your productivity. It is an act of worship to stop, breathe, and delight in Him.

Instead of resisting rest or labeling it laziness, see it as a gift from God. Just as He blessed the seventh day and made it holy, He blesses your obedience to slow down and embrace His rhythm for your life.

SPEAK LIFE: "God's rest is a part of His plan for me."

TALK TO GOD: God, prompt me this week to worship You by resting in You. Amen.

REFLECT & RESPOND: Where have you been running nonstop lately? Write it down, and then pause to rest this week.

DAY 130

Boast About Your Weaknesses

"Each time he said, 'My grace is all you need. My power works best in weakness.' So now I am glad to boast about my weaknesses, so that the power of Christ can work through me."

2 Corinthians 12:9 NLT

Do you ever view your weaknesses as liabilities?

The world teaches us that weakness is failure, and it's a flaw we should hide. However, Paul helps us see another perspective. Our weaknesses are opportunities for Christ's power to be displayed. His power flourishes—and often does its best work through our weaknesses. When we are weak, He is always strong.

This grace-filled truth reminds us it's okay to acknowledge our limits; when we do, God's strength does what we can't. Instead of trying to be enough on our own today, let's remember His grace is all we need. His power makes us sufficient.

Be like Paul. Don't continue to hide your weaknesses; go ahead and boast about them. You understand what others may not. Weakness invites the power of Christ to work through you. In this light, your weaknesses are actually strengths!

SPEAK LIFE: "My weaknesses aren't liabilities; they invite Christ's power."

TALK TO GOD: Lord, when I am weak, remind me in Your grace that You are strong. Amen.

REFLECT & RESPOND: Thank Jesus for His grace today. Pray for His power to meet you in every need.

DAY 131

Trade Striving for Stillness

"But I have calmed and quieted myself, I am like a weaned child with its mother; like a weaned child I am content."

Psalm 131:2 NIV

Are you caught up in a cycle of striving?

The truth is, we weren't designed to strive. It drains us. We push, plan, and hustle, hoping to prove ourselves or secure what we think we need. Yet, David shows us something better: release and rest. Like a child no longer crying for milk, but instead resting quietly in his mother's presence, David's soul is still.

What a countercultural way to live. Instead of chasing after more, David chose contentment in God's care. He didn't demand answers for every mystery or control over every outcome. He simply trusted. We can do the same. When we quiet our hearts before the Lord, the desire to strive diminishes and is replaced by His peace.

Today, allow God to still your soul. Trade the endless cycle of proving and performing for the gentle peace of His presence.

SPEAK LIFE: "I choose stillness over striving today."

TALK TO GOD: Lord God, I trade my striving today for trust. Still my soul today, and show me how I can quiet my heart before You. Amen.

REFLECT & RESPOND: Is there a place in life where you feel the pressure to keep striving? How can you invite God to quiet your soul in that area today?

DAY 132

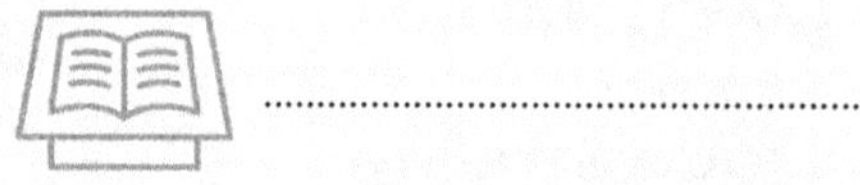

Reflect

Take a few moments to revisit the days you've just walked. There's no rush here—just honesty and grace. Feel free to journal your answers.

Reflection Prompts:

- ✓ What truth stood out to me this week?
- ✓ Where did I notice God inviting me to stop settling?
- ✓ What challenged me? What encouraged me?
- ✓ What thought/encouragement/hope do I want to carry with me into the coming days?

DAY 133

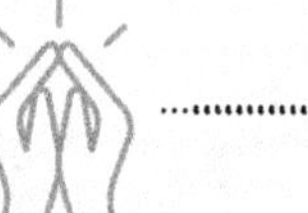

Rest

Today is a day to rest—not to catch up, fix something, or prove anything. Abundant life includes stopping long enough to receive what God is already offering you.

Sit quietly with God for a few minutes.

Breathe deeply.

Allow any Scripture from the past few days to encourage you.

Let yourself be loved and cared for by your Creator.

DAY 134

Live Generously, Live Fully

"The generous will prosper; those who refresh others will themselves be refreshed."

Proverbs 11:25 NLT

What if living generously didn't deplete you— but instead, filled you?

God's kingdom works differently from the world's. The world says to hold tightly, to protect what's ours, and to horde as much as we can for ourselves. God invites us to do the opposite: to open our hands, to give what we've been given, and to trust that He will supply more than what we need.

Generosity isn't just about giving; it's a way of life. It's freely offering our time, encouragement, prayers, forgiveness, and presence. When we refresh others with what we have, we find ourselves refreshed, too. Isn't that just like God? He designed giving not only to bless the recipient. Giving also blesses the giver.

A generous life is a full life, overflowing with God's joy, His purpose, and His blessings. He desires His best for you, which is an abundant, generous life. Be generous with what you have today, refresh others, and live fully.

SPEAK LIFE: "Generosity is my way of life."

TALK TO GOD: Lord, show me who I can be generous with today and how I can refresh another. Amen.

REFLECT & RESPOND: How have you been refreshed after refreshing someone else? What's one simple way you can live generously today?

DAY 135

Trust and Be Faithful

"Trust in the Lord and do good. Then you will live safely in the land and prosper."

Psalm 37:3 NLT

How well are you trusting God in this season of your life?

David wrote these words to people surrounded by wickedness and uncertainty. They could have easily felt unsettled and panicked. Instead of urging them to fret, hide, or control the situation on their own, he called them to trust God and to be faithful right where God had them.

This wisdom is for us today, too. Trust and be faithful. Both of these require action. Trusting God is having confidence that God is at work, even when there's no evidence. Living faithfully is doing good where we are with integrity, kindness, and obedience. These bless others, and they bless God.

When you trust God in the present and live faithfully today, His peace and provision flourish in every area of your life. Today, trust Him over striving on your own. Be faithful where He's placed you. He will bless you in His perfect time.

SPEAK LIFE: "I trust God in every area of my life today."

TALK TO GOD: Lord, help me to trust You in all ways and to live faithfully, doing good today. Amen.

REFLECT & RESPOND: What is one way you can tangibly trust God right now? How will you do good where God has you today?

DAY 136

Run to Win

"Don't you realize that in a race everyone runs, but only one person gets the prize? So run to win! All athletes are disciplined in their training. They do it to win a prize that will fade away, but we do it for an eternal prize."

1 Corinthians 9:24-25 NLT

Do you ever feel it's too difficult to persevere in the race of life?

Like any race, this marathon of your Christian faith requires focus, perseverance, and training. At times, we may be tempted to slow down or give up, but God encourages us to keep running with endurance.

Paul reminds us that our prize isn't a medal or an award. It's eternal life with Jesus, the joy of finishing faithfully, and the reward of hearing Him say one day how we finished our race well.

Today, lift your eyes, steady your pace, and keep pressing forward. Run to win, not striving for perfection; instead fix your eyes on Jesus. He is waiting at the finish line.

SPEAK LIFE: "I fix my eyes on Jesus and run with perseverance."

TALK TO GOD: Lord, when I'm feeling weary or discouraged or questioning if I can go on, strengthen me to run this race, fixing my eyes on You. Amen.

REFLECT & RESPOND: What is tempting you to slow down in your faith race? How will you stay focused on your eternal reward today?

DAY 137

Embrace Your Place

"But you are not like that, for you are a chosen people. You are royal priests, a holy nation, God's very own possession ... 'Once you had no identity as a people; now you are God's people ...'"

1 Peter 2:9–10 NLT

Have you ever walked into a room and wondered if you belonged?

Maybe you felt out of place, overlooked, or unwanted. This ache can make you question your worth and wonder if you'll ever fit in.

Scripture speaks a better truth: you belong to Him. You're not a mistake, not an outsider, not someone He merely tolerates. You are chosen. Wanted. Part of His people with a place, a purpose, and a name.

This belonging rests in what God declares. You may have wandered without identity for a time, but now, you are His.

You hold a seat at His table, a role in His kingdom, and a place in His heart. So, when you feel you don't fit in, remember this: you're not just invited—you're included. Fully. Freely. Forever.

You belong here.

SPEAK LIFE: "I belong to God, and I am invited and included."

TALK TO GOD: God, when I feel out of place, remind me I am Yours and have a special place in Your heart. Amen.

REFLECT & RESPOND: Where do you feel like you don't belong? Surrender this to God and ask Him to remind you where you do belong—right by His side.

DAY 138

Quiet the Inner Critic

"How precious are your thoughts about me, O God. They cannot be numbered!"

Psalm 139:17 NLT

What does your inner critic often say about you?

Most of us carry a voice inside that speaks harshly: pointing out flaws, replaying mistakes, and measuring us by standards God never set. Yet, Psalm 139:17 reminds us of something radically different: God's thoughts about us are precious, countless, and filled with love.

Think about this. While your inner critic presents evidence against you, God speaks affirmation over you. While your mind replays shortcomings, God remembers your true worth. His thoughts aren't negative or critical; they're abundant and full of delight.

The truth is, you don't have to agree with self-criticism. You can choose, instead, to agree with the God who formed you, knows you, and cherishes you more than you can imagine. Allow your thoughts about you to match His.

Today, quiet the inner critic by replacing its lies with God's truth about you. His voice is the declaration of truth.

SPEAK LIFE: "God's thoughts about me are filled with love."

TALK TO GOD: Lord, when I start to self-criticize, silence the voice within and remind me of how You think about me. Amen.

REFLECT & RESPOND: What's the loudest internal message you've been hearing lately? How can you replace it with God's thoughts about you today?

DAY 139

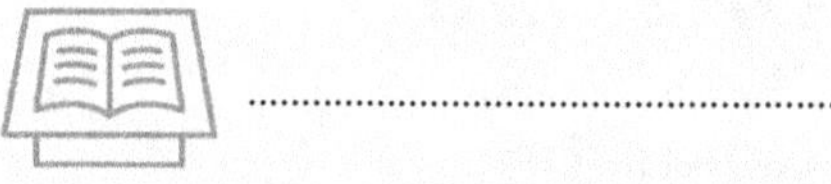

Reflect

Take a few moments to revisit the days you've just walked. There's no rush here—just honesty and grace. Feel free to journal your answers.

Reflection Prompts:

- ✓ What truth stood out to me this week?
- ✓ Where did I notice God inviting me to stop settling?
- ✓ What challenged me? What encouraged me?
- ✓ What thought/encouragement/hope do I want to carry with me into the coming days?

DAY 140

Rest

Today is a day to rest—not to catch up, fix something, or prove anything. Abundant life includes stopping long enough to receive what God is already offering you.

Sit quietly with God for a few minutes.

Breathe deeply.

Allow any Scripture from the past few days to encourage you.

Let yourself be loved and cared for by your Creator.

DAY 141

Trust God's Timing

"Yet God has made everything beautiful for its own time. He has planted eternity in the human heart, but even so, people cannot see the whole scope of God's work from beginning to end."

Ecclesiastes 3:11 NLT

Is waiting uncomfortable for you?

For most, it is. We want answers, results, and breakthroughs—now. Yet, God's timing isn't delayed or rushed. It's perfect. Solomon reminds us that God makes everything beautiful in its time, not in ours.

He sees the beginning and the end, while we only view a piece of the picture. This is why waiting can feel frustrating. We long for the outcome, while God is working deeper behind the scenes. His timing isn't just about when events come to pass. His timing is also preparing our hearts, our faith, and our character to receive what He's planned.

Trusting God's timing requires both patience and trust. It's choosing to believe that even when you can't see His finished work yet, He is aligning things with eternal purpose.

Today, take a breath. God's timing is exactly what you need, exactly when you need it.

SPEAK LIFE: "God's timing is always perfect."

TALK TO GOD: Lord, remind me to wait in trusting obedience, knowing You're working where I can't see yet. Amen.

REFLECT & RESPOND: Where do you feel most impatient right now? How might God be using this wait to prepare you for His perfect plan?

DAY 142

Return When Faith Feels Dry

"The Lord will guide you continually, giving you water when you are dry and restoring your strength. You will be like a well-watered garden, like an ever-flowing spring."

Isaiah 58:11 NLT

Are you in a season where your faith feels flat or dry?

Maybe it feels empty or weary. Possibly the excitement of walking closely with God has faded, and your prayers sound hollow or repetitive. If so, you might begin to wonder, *What's wrong with me? Where is God now?*

You're not alone if this is where you are today. Even the most faithful ones experience faith-fading seasons. The good news is that God doesn't retreat if you ever do. He meets you, even in the middle of the drought—nourishing, strengthening, and reviving what feels weak and barren.

This promise from Isaiah is timely. A well-watered garden doesn't thrive on one rainfall; it's sustained by a continual flow. God doesn't promise a one-time fill; He instead offers an abundant spring of living water for your thirsty soul.

Return to Him, even in the dryness. Especially in the dryness. He's offering strength and refreshment right here, right now.

SPEAK LIFE: "God refreshes my soul, even when I feel empty."

TALK TO GOD: God, when my faith feels dry, remind me You are my abundant source. Amen.

REFLECT & RESPOND: What has your faith felt like lately— vibrant or dry? Invite God to water the dry places in your soul.

DAY 143

Choose What's Better

"'Martha, Martha,' the Lord answered, 'you are worried and upset about many things, but few things are needed—or indeed only one. Mary has chosen what is better, and it will not be taken away from her.'"

Luke 10:41-42 NIV

Does your life ever feel full of half-finished projects, too many commitments, and numerous good intentions—all demanding attention at the same time?

Martha likely knew this feeling. She was concerned about serving, preparing, and doing good work, but Jesus pointed her to something better: being present with Him.

This invitation is for us today, too. This doesn't mean to abandon our responsibilities, but instead, let our priorities flow from the one thing that matters most: Jesus. When we choose Him over what seems urgent or important, we're aligning our day with what Jesus says is most essential. This simplifies everything, even when life feels too full.

Pause and ask: *What matters most in this moment?* Then choose it. Even small shifts in attention toward prayer, loving someone well, or listening for God's voice can turn a distracted day into a sacred one.

SPEAK LIFE: "I choose what's most important today: Jesus."

TALK TO GOD: Lord God, I desire a sacred life over a scattered one. Guide me to put You first in my thoughts, my actions, and my life. Amen.

REFLECT & RESPOND: What's one distraction you can lay aside today? How can you create more space for Jesus?

DAY 144

Use Praise as Your Weapon

"May the praise of God be in their mouths and a double-edged sword in their hands ..."

Psalm 149:6 NIV

Have you ever considered praise as a weapon?

This verse paints a powerful picture of praise in our mouths and a sword in our hands. It reminds us that praise isn't just reserved for Sunday morning; it's mighty in life's battles. When we declare God's goodness and faithfulness out loud, we expel fear, doubt, and discouragement.

Praise doesn't deny what's difficult, but it conveys a bolder truth: that God is faithful, strong, and victorious. With Him on our side, His victory is ours. Just as a sword defends and protects, praise cuts through the lies of the enemy and recenters us in God's presence.

When life's battles feel overwhelming, this is your reminder to not stay silent. Lift your voice in praise. Let your worship of God be both your strength and your defense. With His Word in your hand and His praise on your lips, you already stand in triumph.

SPEAK LIFE: "I choose to praise God when facing life's battles."

TALK TO GOD: Lord, instead of being silent in whatever trials I face, remind me to praise You in the midst of them. Amen.

REFLECT & RESPOND: How can you praise God through the challenges you're facing now? Write your praises down to see them in black and white.

DAY 145

See Your Body as Good

"You made all the delicate, inner parts of my body and knit me together in my mother's womb. Thank you for making me so wonderfully complex! Your workmanship is marvelous— how well I know it."

Psalm 139:13-14 NLT

How do you generally perceive your body?

Your body is special. It tells a story—not just of genetics or family history, but also of God's design, care, and purpose. Every scar, stretch mark, and wrinkle is part of something greater. Some marks remind you of victories won, others of pain endured. All of them bear witness to God's caring and steady hand.

The world says your body is only valuable if it looks a certain way or is a certain size. God's Word says something different: your body was knit together by Him, an intricate, marvelous work. Even the parts you might want to hide are known, seen, and loved by your Creator.

When you view your body through His eyes, you'll see a vessel of His story, carrying His Spirit, designed to glorify Him in every season. See your body as good.

SPEAK LIFE: "God created my body, and it is good."

TALK TO GOD: Heavenly Father, help me to see my body as You see it: Your amazing creation. Amen.

REFLECT & RESPOND: What part of your body tells a story of God's faithfulness? How can you thank Him for it today?

DAY 146

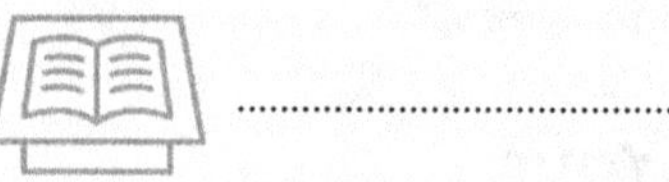

Reflect

Take a few moments to revisit the days you've just walked. There's no rush here—just honesty and grace. Feel free to journal your answers.

Reflection Prompts:

- ✓ What truth stood out to me this week?
- ✓ Where did I notice God inviting me to stop settling?
- ✓ What challenged me? What encouraged me?
- ✓ What thought/encouragement/hope do I want to carry with me into the coming days?

DAY 147

Rest

Today is a day to rest—not to catch up, fix something, or prove anything. Abundant life includes stopping long enough to receive what God is already offering you.

Sit quietly with God for a few minutes.

Breathe deeply.

Allow any Scripture from the past few days to encourage you.

Let yourself be loved and cared for by your Creator.

DAY 148

Rest
Well
Tonight

"I lie down and sleep; I wake again, because the Lord sustains me."

Psalm 3:5 NIV

What thoughts keep you awake at night?

Sleep is a vulnerable act, isn't it? We close our eyes, release control, and trust that we'll wake to a new day. For David, surrounded by enemies and uncertainty, sleep was a step of faith. He could rest because he trusted the Lord to watch over him and sustain him.

The same is true for you. No matter what burdens overwhelm or what worries weigh heavily, you can lie down in peace knowing God won't leave you—not for one moment. He is present through the night, guarding you, restoring you, and blessing you.

Rest is fully trusting God, the One who is in control and the One who sustains. Each morning you wake is living proof of His faithfulness—a reminder that He carried you through the night and will carry you through this day, too.

Tonight, lay down your heavy burdens. Trust your Heavenly Father Who never slumbers so that you can. Rest well, friend.

SPEAK LIFE: "Trusting God to protect and sustain me helps me rest well."

TALK TO GOD: Lord, remind me when I'm struggling to rest that You're in control, and I don't have to be. Amen.

REFLECT & RESPOND: What keeps you from resting well at night? Will you surrender this to God and ask Him to sustain you?

DAY 149

Speak Life, Live Fully

"The tongue can bring death or life; those who love to talk will reap the consequences."

Proverbs 18:21 NLT

Do you ever consider the power of your speech?

Words shape worlds. What you speak matters. Every word sows seeds in your heart and into the lives of others. Your words carry the power to either build or break, to bless or burden. When you speak words of life, you partner with God in creating an atmosphere of hope, faith, and abundance.

This isn't about blindly saying everything is perfect. It's about choosing to align your voice with God's truth instead of your fears, frustrations, or doubts. When you declare His promises, when you encourage instead of complain, when you bless instead of criticize, you create space for His fullness to flourish.

The life you long for begins right here, with the words on your tongue. Speak life over your circumstances. Speak life over your family. Speak life over yourself. Then watch how God uses these words to bring His abundance to life.

SPEAK LIFE: "Today I will speak words that align with God's truth."

TALK TO GOD: Lord, align my words with Yours today, and help me speak life over myself and others. Amen.

REFLECT & RESPOND: What words have you spoken recently that were life draining? What's one truth from God's Word you can speak over your life today?

DAY 150

Use Your Unique Gifts

"In his grace, God has given us different gifts for doing certain things well."

Romans 12:6a NLT

Have you ever wished your gifts looked more like someone else's?

God gave you gifts on purpose, and they aren't designed to look like anyone else's. He designed the body of Christ with unique members, each one valuable and necessary. Your assignment is yours alone, crafted with your strengths, experiences, and calling in mind.

It's tempting to compare—to measure our gifts against hers, to wonder if ours are enough, or to wish for a different role. This kind of comparison only distracts us from following the assignment God has given us. If your gift is encouraging, encourage boldly. If it's teaching, teach faithfully. If it's giving, give generously. God doesn't expect you to do her work, but instead be faithful only to yours.

God's kingdom doesn't need counterfeit copies; it needs you. When you walk fully in your God-given assignment, you not only glorify Him, but you also bless those who need what only you can offer.

SPEAK LIFE: "My God-given gift is needed in this world."

TALK TO GOD: Lord, thank You for the gifts You have given me. May I use them for Your glory and for the good of others. Amen.

REFLECT & RESPOND: How are you tempted to compare your gifts with someone else's? What if you, instead, saw your role as uniquely irreplaceable in God's plan?

DAY 151

Don't Give Up Doing Good

"So let's not get tired of doing what is good. At just the right time we will reap a harvest of blessing if we don't give up."

Galatians 6:9 NLT

Do you ever get tired of doing what's good?

Sometimes it feels like no one notices, or the results seem slow in coming. Other times, it feels as if doing good is like swimming upstream.

The truth is that God sees every effort, hears every prayer, and knows every act of kindness. Paul encourages us that there is a harvest waiting—one that comes from His perfect timing.

This is when perseverance and faith in action, matter. It's choosing to keep going when quitting would be easier. It's clinging to God's promises even when the evidence isn't visible yet. It's also trusting that He is weaving your faithfulness into something beautiful you may not see this side of eternity.

Don't give up doing good. Keep showing up. Your steady faith is planting seeds that will one day bloom into blessings.

SPEAK LIFE: "I keep doing good, even if the results are not visible."

TALK TO GOD: God, prompt me to keep going today, knowing that persevering in doing good matters. I trust the timing of Your blessing. Amen.

REFLECT & RESPOND: Where are you tempted to give up right now? How can you lean on God's strength instead of your own as you keep going?

DAY 152

Listen for the Whisper

"And after the earthquake there was a fire, but the Lord was not in the fire. And after the fire there was the sound of a gentle whisper."

1 Kings 19:12 NLT

When recently have you made space to be still with God?

We might expect God to speak through big, bold, unmistakable moments—lightning bolts, burning bushes, or mountaintops. Sometimes, though, God chooses the quietest voice: a whisper. That's what Elijah discovered in the cave after the extensive elements had passed. God wasn't in the wind, the earthquake, or the fire. He was in the quiet stillness.

God's whisper requires our stillness, too. Not necessarily still bodies, but rather still hearts. A calm soul. A demeanor that's poised to listen, not just speak. We miss His voice when we're rushing through our days, bombarded by noise and distraction. However, when we make space for silence, even for a few minutes, His whisper comes through clearly.

God isn't hiding. He's not silent. He's just often quieter than we expect—and nearer than we know. Find moments to be still and listen for His voice today.

SPEAK LIFE: "I will listen for God's whisper in moments of stillness today."

TALK TO GOD: God, still my heart right now, enough to hear Your voice. Amen.

REFLECT & RESPOND: How long has it been since you sat in silence, expecting to hear from God? What can you do today to better hear His whisper?

DAY 153

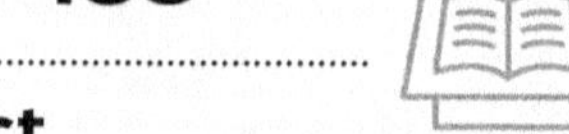

Reflect

Take a few moments to revisit the days you've just walked. There's no rush here—just honesty and grace. Feel free to journal your answers.

Reflection Prompts:

- ✓ What truth stood out to me this week?
- ✓ Where did I notice God inviting me to stop settling?
- ✓ What challenged me? What encouraged me?
- ✓ What thought/encouragement/hope do I want to carry with me into the coming days?

DAY 154

Rest

Today is a day to rest—not to catch up, fix something, or prove anything. Abundant life includes stopping long enough to receive what God is already offering you.

Sit quietly with God for a few minutes.

Breathe deeply.

Allow any Scripture from the past few days to encourage you.

Let yourself be loved and cared for by your Creator.

DAY 155

Remain Hopeful in Your Tears

"'…He will wipe every tear from their eyes, and there will be no more death or sorrow or crying or pain. All these things are gone forever.'"

Revelation 21:4 NLT

Has life caused you tears recently?

Since we live in a broken world, it's no wonder we experience brokenness and heartache. Sorrow, pain, grief, or loss can cause tears to well up within us. The promise John declares is that one day death, sorrow, crying, and pain will no longer exist. *Can you fathom this?*

Imagine the tender hand of God wiping away every tear from your eyes. No more sickness. No more funerals. No more broken relationships. No more aching bodies or weary souls. Instead, perfect peace, wholeness, and joy forever in His presence. It'll be wonderful, won't it?

This hope does not remove today's pain, no, but it does transform how you endure it. Today, live fully, knowing suffering is temporary, and heaven's healing is eternal.

SPEAK LIFE: "In sorrow, I remember God will wipe away every tear."

TALK TO GOD: Lord, thank You for the reminder that You will one day remove all tears, sorrow, and pain. In the meantime, help me live with enduring hope. Amen.

REFLECT & RESPOND: What sorrows or struggles are causing tears in your life today? How does the promise of God wiping away every tear bring you comfort right now?

DAY 156

Cling to Your Anchor

"This hope is a strong and trustworthy anchor for our souls. It leads us through the curtain into God's inner sanctuary."

Hebrews 6:19 NLT

Has life tossed you around lately?

When the winds of uncertainty blow and weariness follows, you might feel like you're drifting out of control. A diagnosis. A job loss. A broken relationship. Even daily demands can feel overwhelming. Here's God's promise to cling to: hope in Jesus is an anchor for your soul.

An anchor doesn't remove the storm, but it holds the ship steady in it, helping it stay secure and safe. That's what hope in Jesus does. It calms your heart when anxiety presses. It stills your mind when doubts swirl. It holds you firm when circumstances threaten your peace.

This hope is grounded in the faithfulness of God, sealed by His promises, and secured by the cross and empty tomb. It points beyond today's trouble to the certainty of eternity with Him.

When everything else feels uncertain, remember: Jesus is your anchor. Cling to Him today. He holds you steady.

SPEAK LIFE: "My hope in Jesus secures me in life's storms."

TALK TO GOD: God, when I'm feeling tossed around in life's storms, remind me that Jesus holds me securely. Amen.

REFLECT & RESPOND: Where in your life do you feel tossed about by uncertainty or fear? How can you cling to Jesus as your anchor today?

DAY 157

Stop Wondering if You Matter

"What is the price of two sparrows—one copper coin? But not a single sparrow can fall to the ground without your Father knowing it. And the very hairs on your head are all numbered. So don't be afraid; you are more valuable to God than a whole flock of sparrows."

Matthew 10:29-31 NLT

Do you ever wonder if you really matter to God?

Jesus lovingly declares here that nothing escapes the Father's attention—not even a single sparrow falling. Then He goes further: He knows the very number of hairs on your head.

This isn't some random detail. It's His intimate care. It's His intentional love. It's God saying, *I see every part of you, and you matter deeply to Me.*

You don't have to strive to be noticed or prove your worth. You are already more valuable than an entire flock of sparrows!

So when opinions surround you, or insecurity starts to whisper, claim this truth: Your worth isn't earned. It's established by the One who knows the number of hairs on your head.

Walk today in quiet confidence. You are held. You are known. You are treasured.

SPEAK LIFE: "I am valuable to God. I am His."

TALK TO GOD: Lord, remind me today that I'm valuable because I am Yours. Amen.

REFLECT & RESPOND: Where are you pressured to prove your worth? How does God's view encourage you?

DAY 158

Just Be Willing

"'… I take joy in doing your will, my God, for your instructions are written on my heart.'"

Psalm 40:8 NLT

Are you willing to trust God, even when His plans are unclear?

Sometimes the most beautiful moment is one of surrender, when we can't see or understand God's will. A woman with hands open and a heart willing is one that God can use in powerful ways.

We don't always know what's next, do we? Sometimes God's direction looks blurry, or our fear keeps us from stepping forward with Him. Yet, when we follow, even before we know all the details, we show Him that we trust Him more than our need for understanding.

David's words in this psalm reflect a willing heart—a desire not just to obey, but also to joyfully do God's will. This kind of delight grows when we draw close to God, when we read and apply His Word, and when we place our lives daily in His hands.

Today, just be willing. God can do so much with a heart that says, "I trust You."

SPEAK LIFE: "I delight in doing God's will today."

TALK TO GOD: God, teach me to trust Your will with open hands and a willing heart. Amen.

REFLECT & RESPOND: Where are you struggling in trusting God right now? Share this with Him, and ask Him to help you with surrendering.

DAY 159

Live Mindfully

"So be careful how you live. Don't live like fools, but like those who are wise. Make the most of every opportunity in these evil days."

Ephesians 5:15-16 NLT

Do you ever feel like life is slipping past you?

Days blur into weeks, weeks into years, and suddenly we wonder where the time went. Paul urges us to wake up and to live with purpose, not drift in distraction.

When we live mindfully, we notice God's nudges, the small blessings, and even the ordinary moments He weaves into our days. We pause long enough to ask, *Does this choice, word, or habit draw me closer to Jesus—or away from Him?*

We know we can't control every detail of life, but it is our choice to be present in each one. Living mindfully involves making the most of the time we've been given, aligning our steps with God's purposes.

This kind of intentional living allows us to not just get through the day, but it encourages us to fully embrace the day He's placed before us.

SPEAK LIFE: "I will live wisely, stay present, and thrive in the blessing of today."

TALK TO GOD: God, I don't want to look back and wonder where the time went. Help me to be mindful of the life You've given me. Amen.

REFLECT & RESPOND: Where have you been living on autopilot lately? How can you be fully present and intentional today?

DAY 160

Reflect

Take a few moments to revisit the days you've just walked. There's no rush here—just honesty and grace. Feel free to journal your answers.

Reflection Prompts:

- ✓ What truth stood out to me this week?
- ✓ Where did I notice God inviting me to stop settling?
- ✓ What challenged me? What encouraged me?
- ✓ What thought/encouragement/hope do I want to carry with me into the coming days?

DAY 161

Rest

Today is a day to rest—not to catch up, fix something, or prove anything. Abundant life includes stopping long enough to receive what God is already offering you.

Sit quietly with God for a few minutes.

Breathe deeply.

Allow any Scripture from the past few days to encourage you.

Let yourself be loved and cared for by your Creator.

DAY 162

Thank God in Advance

"Enter his gates with thanksgiving; go into his courts with praise. Give thanks to him and praise his name."

Psalm 100:4 NLT

When was the last time you thanked God in advance?

We are naturally thankful when the prayer is answered or the breakthrough arrives. What about when we're still waiting? The Psalmist invites us to enter God's presence with thanksgiving—not just after we see His provision, but also before we receive it.

Giving thanks before the breakthrough is a beautiful act of faith. It declares, "God, I trust You even though I can't yet see the outcome." It shifts your stance from anxious straining to peaceful confidence, centering on God's unchanging character.

Choosing gratitude now is intentionally embracing the truth that God's goodness is not dependent on what you see or what happens next. You're inviting His presence into your present moment, which changes everything, even before your circumstances do.

Today, step into His gates with thanksgiving, believing that He's already at work in ways you can't yet see. Because He is.

SPEAK LIFE: "I thank God for working in my life, even if I can't see results yet."

TALK TO GOD: God, I thank You in advance for my breakthrough. I trust You and have full confidence in You. Amen.

REFLECT & RESPOND: What can you thank God for in advance today? How might gratitude change your outlook while you wait?

DAY 163

Steward, Don't Strive

"His master replied, 'Well done, good and faithful servant! You have been faithful with a few things; I will put you in charge of many things. Come and share your master's happiness!'"

Matthew 25:23 NIV

Do you ever get striving and stewardship confused?

They may look similar on the outside, but their origins are completely different. Striving is fueled by pressure: the need to please, achieve, or earn approval. Stewarding is fueled by purpose: taking care of what God has given you.

When you strive, you carry the weight yourself. When you steward, God helps bear the load. One drains you; the other sustains you. In God's kingdom, success isn't measured by hustle; it's measured by faithfulness. As Matthew indicates, your role is to simply and faithfully use the time, talents, and resources God has placed in your hands and trust Him with the outcome.

You can release the exhausting urge to do more just to feel worthy or accepted. Instead, honor God by taking care of what you already have, knowing that faithfulness, not frantic effort, is what He celebrates.

SPEAK LIFE: "Striving drains me, while stewarding sustains me."

TALK TO GOD: God, remind me to faithfully steward what You have given me. Help me to honor You. Amen.

REFLECT & RESPOND: Where have you been striving instead of stewarding? How might God be inviting you to live differently?

DAY 164

Be Content in God's Provision

"Yet true godliness with contentment is itself great wealth. After all, we brought nothing with us when we came into the world, and we can't take anything with us when we leave it. So if we have enough food and clothing, let us be content."

1 Timothy 6:6-8 NLT

Do you ever struggle with contentment?

Our culture teaches that accumulation equals abundance. We may think we'll be happy with more—more stuff, success, recognition, or money. Yet, Scripture highlights a different truth: enough really is enough.

Godliness with contentment is described as great wealth because it reminds us what truly matters. When we stop striving for what we don't have, we begin to see the blessing of what we already do. The roof over our head, the food on our table, the clothes on our back—all are evidence of God's faithful provision.

Living in this kind of contentment keeps us grateful. We are no longer enticed to compare and to strive. We find ourselves living lighter and with more joy. In God's hands, enough is always enough.

SPEAK LIFE: "God's faithful provision is all I need."

TALK TO GOD: Lord, thank You for Your provision. When I am tempted to want more, remind me that You provide all I need. Amen.

REFLECT & RESPOND: Where do you feel the pull of wanting more in your life? How might practicing gratitude today help you embrace enough?

DAY 165

Make Your Words Count

"And I tell you this, you must give an account on judgment day for every idle word you speak. The words you say will either acquit you or condemn you."'

Matthew 12:36-37 NLT

What if you considered every word important?

Each word leaves a trace, either positive or negative. Our words can heal wounds, offer hope, and strengthen faith, but they can also wound, discourage, and mislead. God reminds us that what we say matters, and He holds us accountable for our words.

This isn't to instill fear, but instead to empower responsibility and intentionality. Before speaking, it's always wise to pause and ask, *Will this build up or tear down? Does it reflect God's truth or my feelings?* Choosing life-giving words reshapes relationships, perspectives, and even your own heart.

Your voice is a tool of influence. Through it, you're given the opportunity to bring encouragement to overcome doubt, hope to eliminate despair, and peace to replace chaos. Allow your words to honor God, strengthen others, and invite His life-giving work in every interaction.

SPEAK LIFE: "My words bring life to me and others today."

TALK TO GOD: Lord, keep a guard over my mouth to speak only what's encouraging and hopeful. Help me to speak life. Amen.

REFLECT & RESPOND: Thinking back over your words recently, which ones were life-giving? What's one specific word or phrase you can speak today that reflects God's truth?

DAY 166

Look for God in the Middle

"The Lord replied, 'My Presence will go with you, and I will give you rest.'"

Exodus 33:14 NIV

Is the journey feeling long, difficult, or uncertain?

Are you questioning where God is? You might not be where you used to be, but you're not yet where you hope to be either. You're in the middle. The middle can feel messy, confusing, and lonely. It's also where God's presence often meets you most intimately.

He's not yet waiting for you at the finish line, nor is He lingering in the past. He is with you right now—right in the in-between. When Moses was leading the Israelites through the wilderness, he asked God for reassurance. God answered him, not with a promise of a pain-free path, but rather with the promise of His presence. This is still His promise for you today.

When you feel overwhelmed or unsure, remember: God's presence is what keeps you steady and secure. He's with you, strengthening you. He's guiding you and will never leave you. Yes, even here—even now—you are not alone in the messy middle. Look for Him today.

SPEAK LIFE: "God is with me, even in this messy middle."

TALK TO GOD: God, I trust You are with me even now through the middle places of life. Amen.

REFLECT & RESPOND: What part of your journey feels like "the middle"? How can you surrender it to God and find rest today?

DAY 167

Reflect

Take a few moments to revisit the days you've just walked. There's no rush here—just honesty and grace. Feel free to journal your answers.

Reflection Prompts:

- ✓ What truth stood out to me this week?
- ✓ Where did I notice God inviting me to stop settling?
- ✓ What challenged me? What encouraged me?
- ✓ What thought/encouragement/hope do I want to carry with me into the coming days?

DAY 168

Rest

Today is a day to rest—not to catch up, fix something, or prove anything. Abundant life includes stopping long enough to receive what God is already offering you.

Sit quietly with God for a few minutes.

Breathe deeply.

Allow any Scripture from the past few days to encourage you.

Let yourself be loved and cared for by your Creator.

DAY 169

Give Without Expectation

"But love your enemies, do good to them, and lend to them without expecting to get anything back. Then your reward will be great, and you will be children of the Most High, because he is kind to the ungrateful and wicked."

Luke 6:35 NIV

Is it easier to give knowing you'll receive something in return?

Maybe you're promised gratitude, recognition, or an even exchange. Yet, Jesus reframes this human instinct. He invites us to give—not to gain—to reflect the generous love of our Father. God gives freely every single day, even to those who ignore Him or reject Him.

When we release the expectation of repayment, we also release resentment, disappointment, and hidden strings attached to our generosity. Instead of keeping score, we trust God will honor it in His way, in His time. Giving without expectancy frees us to love like Jesus: open-handed, unconditional, and without limits.

This kind of giving isn't easy, especially to someone considered an enemy. It stretches us, and it requires the Holy Spirit to change our hearts. The work is worth it. Give without expectation today.

SPEAK LIFE: "I will give freely without expectation."

TALK TO GOD: Lord, do a mighty work in my heart to give without expecting anything in return and to trust You with my giving. Amen.

REFLECT & RESPOND: When have you recently expected something in return for your generosity? How will you practice giving freely today?

DAY 170

Keep Your Eyes on Jesus

"We do this by keeping our eyes on Jesus, the champion who initiates and perfects our faith. Because of the joy awaiting him, he endured the cross, disregarding its shame. Now he is seated in the place of honor beside God's throne."

Hebrews 12:2 NLT

Have you lost your focus?

It's easy to do when life pulls us in many directions. Distractions such as packed schedules, health struggles, or even good things can quietly steal our gaze away from Jesus. We can't run the race of faith effectively with divided attention.

Hebrews 12 reminds us that Jesus is both the beginning and the finisher of our faith. He is our example of endurance: facing the cross, not with dread, but rather joy, knowing what was to come. When our eyes stay fixed on Him, we find the strength to keep moving forward, even when the path feels long and steep.

Keeping our eyes on Jesus means staying focused on the One who knows the way, sets the pace, and carries us when we grow weary. With our focus on Him, we don't just finish the race, we finish well.

SPEAK LIFE: "My eyes stay fixed on Jesus."

TALK TO GOD: Lord, when distractions arise, help me to keep my eyes on You. Amen.

REFLECT & RESPOND: What distractions shift your focus away from Jesus? How can you practically fix your eyes on Him today?

DAY 171

Don't Delay, Obey

"Remember, it is sin to know what you ought to do and then not do it."

James 4:17 NLT

When have you delayed obedience out of fear, pride, or uncertainty?

When God calls us into obedience, the calling is not for later. It's not something we can put on hold until it feels right. When God asks us to do something, whether it's forgiving someone, giving generously, or stepping into a new calling, He desires us to follow through—now.

We might tell ourselves we'll obey when we're more ready, when we understand more, or when the timing seems better. As James tells us, delayed obedience is really disobedience in disguise. In the delay, we miss out on the blessings that come from walking in step with God right now.

God's commands aren't meant to be burdensome; they're meant to bless you with His best. When He prompts your heart, trust Him enough to say yes without delay. Immediate obedience is the evidence of your trusting heart.

SPEAK LIFE: "When God calls me to do something, I will do it immediately."

TALK TO GOD: Lord, when I'm tempted to delay following Your call, remind me that delayed obedience is disobedience. Amen.

REFLECT & RESPOND: Is there an area where you've been delaying obedience to God? What step can you take today to respond in faith without hesitation?

DAY 172

Declare Overwhelming Victory

"No, despite all these things, overwhelming victory is ours through Christ, who loved us."

Romans 8:37 NLT

Have you felt defeated lately?

This world often determines victory by outward success—winning the award, achieving the dream, solving the problem. Yet, Paul helps us see that, in Christ, our victory is much deeper. It's not just survival or scraping by; it's *overwhelming* victory.

Paul's words didn't flow from an easy life. His life was full of hardship, persecution, and struggle. His confidence was unwavering, as nothing—not trouble, fear, or death—could separate him from Jesus' love. This same love is the reason we are victorious.

Thankfully, your victory doesn't rely on you, your strength, resources, or performance. It relies on Jesus, Who already won the battle through the cross and His resurrection. Because He overcame, you overcome. Because He is victorious, you are victorious.

When the enemy whispers defeat or when life feels overwhelming, declare this truth: victory belongs to you in Jesus. Walk boldly in it. Live freely because of it. The battle has been decided, and His love has won.

SPEAK LIFE: "In Jesus, I have overwhelming victory."

TALK TO GOD: Lord, thank You that Your victory is mine. Help me remember this when I feel defeated, overwhelmed, or overcome. Amen.

REFLECT & RESPOND: When have you been tempted to live defeated lately? How can you accept that Jesus' victory is already yours?

DAY 173

Live Like You're Loved

"See what great love the Father has lavished on us, that we should be called children of God! And that is what we are!"

1 John 3:1a NIV

What if you lived today as if you were truly loved?

Instead of questioning your worthiness, what if you embraced the truth of God's deep and lasting love for you? Not trying to gain His approval. Not striving to earn it. But receiving it, resting in it, and living from it—because He loves you, His daughter.

God doesn't love you only on your best days or merely puts up with you on your worst. His love for you is constant and complete. He lavishes it—pouring it out generously and without limit.

When you live like you're loved, something changes. You stop trying to earn love, and you start walking in the purpose God has for you. You show up authentically. You love others freely. You speak truth with grace. You trust Him without fear of rejection.

The next time you start to question your worth, pause and remember: you are already lavishly loved.

SPEAK LIFE: "I am deeply loved by God."

TALK TO GOD: Lord, when I begin to question Your love, prompt me to remember Your truth in this Scripture. Amen.

REFLECT & RESPOND: What's one way you can live like you're loved today? Who in your life also needs this truth?

DAY 174

Reflect

Take a few moments to revisit the days you've just walked. There's no rush here—just honesty and grace. Feel free to journal your answers.

Reflection Prompts:

- ✓ What truth stood out to me this week?
- ✓ Where did I notice God inviting me to stop settling?
- ✓ What challenged me? What encouraged me?
- ✓ What thought/encouragement/hope do I want to carry with me into the coming days?

DAY 175

Rest

Today is a day to rest—not to catch up, fix something, or prove anything. Abundant life includes stopping long enough to receive what God is already offering you.

Sit quietly with God for a few minutes.

Breathe deeply.

Allow any Scripture from the past few days to encourage you.

Let yourself be loved and cared for by your Creator.

DAY 176

Trade the Mask for Mercy

"Confess your sins to each other and pray for each other so that you may be healed. The earnest prayer of a righteous person has great power and produces wonderful results."

James 5:16 NLT

What kind of mask have you recently worn?

We sometimes put on masks, don't we? Not the costume kind, but rather the "I'm fine" or the "everything's perfect" kind. Maybe it's the confident look, the successful accolades, or the polished personality, disguising private pain.

Wearing masks may protect us from others' judgment, but they can also prevent us from healing. James points us to a different way: a way of prayer, not pretending. Healing, not hiding. When we dare to be real—with safe people and before God—we lift the cover and open ourselves to compassion.

Healing begins when we remove the mask and trade it for God's mercy. We exchange pretending for prayer, and allow grace to touch the places we've kept hidden too long.

You no longer have to hide or pretend. Just be honest, and trust that God's mercy will meet you right where you are, right when you need it.

SPEAK LIFE: "I allow myself to be real before God."

TALK TO GOD: Lord, help me to stop hiding or pretending with You to welcome Your healing into my life. Amen.

REFLECT & RESPOND: Where have you been hiding behind a mask lately? What would it look like to trade that mask for mercy today?

DAY 177

Live a Life of Worship

"And so, dear brothers and sisters, I plead with you to give your bodies to God because of all he has done for you. Let them be a living and holy sacrifice—the kind he will find acceptable. This is truly the way to worship him."

Romans 12:1 NLT

How do you define worship?

It's not confined to Sunday mornings or your favorite playlist, and it's certainly more than a song. Apostle Paul reminds us that true worship is this: offering your whole life—your time, your actions, your thoughts—as a living sacrifice to God. Each moment can become worship when it's offered to Him.

Every task can be done with a heart of worship: folding laundry, making dinner, paying bills, or even running errands. When we live with this kind of attitude in everyday life, we begin to reflect the One we worship.

God delights in your song, yes, but He also delights in your surrendered life, which may look like sorting socks some days. He sees your everyday offerings and calls them beautiful.

SPEAK LIFE: "My life is an offering of worship to God."

TALK TO GOD: Lord, lead me to give my entire being to You. Guide me to live a life of worship. Amen.

REFLECT & RESPOND: What might it look like for you to worship with your life today? Is there some part that God may be inviting you to surrender?

DAY 178

Open the Gift of Today

"How do you know what your life will be like tomorrow? Your life is like the morning fog—it's here a little while, then it's gone."

James 4:14 NLT

Have you ever paused to consider that today might be all you have?

We often plan for tomorrow as if it's guaranteed, but Scripture reminds us that every day we wake up is a gift. Life is fragile and fleeting, and while that can feel sobering, it's also an invitation to live gratefully right now.

When we realize tomorrow isn't promised, our priorities adjust. We hug tighter, speak kinder, love bolder, and choose what matters over what merely fills the time. Gratitude becomes more than a feeling; it becomes a way of life.

God, in His grace, has placed you right here, right now, for a reason. You're alive in this unique, God-gifted moment. Instead of letting the hours slip by unnoticed, receive them as priceless, unique gifts.

You've been given today. Live it fully, love others well, and leave no moment wasted.

SPEAK LIFE: "I cherish God's gift of today and live fully in it."

TALK TO GOD: God, please realign my priorities where needed, and help me be grateful in every moment. Amen.

REFLECT & RESPOND: What is one way you can honor the gift of today? How will you live differently because of it?

DAY 179

Rejoice Even When You Don't Feel Thankful

"Though the fig tree does not bud and there are no grapes on the vines, though the olive crop fails and the fields produce no food, though there are no sheep in the pen and no cattle in the stalls, yet I will rejoice in the Lord, I will be joyful in God my Savior."

Habakkuk 3:17-18 NIV

What do you do when you don't feel thankful?

Life is full of real losses, heavy disappointments, and unanswered prayers. Habakkuk understood this. Emptiness and lack surrounded Him, yet he chose thankfulness and rejoiced in the Lord.

This kind of thankfulness says, *God, You are still worthy, even when my circumstances aren't what I hoped.* It's not faking everything is fine; it's acknowledging that God is still good in the midst of what doesn't look or feel good.

When you can't be thankful *for* everything, you can still be thankful *in* everything. Gratitude in difficulties is a declaration that your hope is grounded in what's eternal, not what's temporary.

Today, trust God in your circumstances, and declare you will continue to rejoice in Him.

SPEAK LIFE: "No matter what, I rejoice in God my Savior."

TALK TO GOD: Lord, help me to rejoice in You, even when I don't feel thankful. Amen.

REFLECT & RESPOND: In what situation are you feeling less than thankful today? How can your gratitude be grounded in God, not your circumstances?

DAY 180

Refuse to Believe Numbers Define You

"And the very hairs on your head are all numbered. So don't be afraid; you are more valuable to God than a whole flock of sparrows."

Luke 12:7 NLT

Do the numbers in your life affect how you define your worth?

Maybe the scale or something else whispers that you're too much, not enough, or failing somehow. We often reduce our value to numbers—pounds, sizes, calories, likes, or followers.

Yet, Jesus confirms this truth: your Heavenly Father knows you so intimately that He's counted every hair on your head. If He cares for sparrows, how much more does He care for you? Your worth isn't based on measurements or statistics; it's defined by His love.

Every scar, curve, and detail tells a story of His perfect craftsmanship. He sees you, knows you, and considers you His priceless daughter. Let that sink in.

When negative thoughts try to reduce you to a number, hold onto this truth: you are infinitely valuable because of your Creator. Walk today in freedom, and let His perspective shape how you see yourself.

SPEAK LIFE: "God sees me, loves me, and delights in me."

TALK TO GOD: God, I'm defined by You. Help me to see myself how You see me. Amen.

REFLECT & RESPOND: Write down the number, size, or weight that has made you feel defined or limited. Then write next to it how God sees you.

DAY 181

Reflect

Take a few moments to revisit the days you've just walked. There's no rush here—just honesty and grace. Feel free to journal your answers.

Reflection Prompts:

- ✓ What truth stood out to me this week?
- ✓ Where did I notice God inviting me to stop settling?
- ✓ What challenged me? What encouraged me?
- ✓ What thought/encouragement/hope do I want to carry with me into the coming days?

DAY 182

Rest

Today is a day to rest—not to catch up, fix something, or prove anything. Abundant life includes stopping long enough to receive what God is already offering you.

Sit quietly with God for a few minutes.

Breathe deeply.

Allow any Scripture from the past few days to encourage you.

Let yourself be loved and cared for by your Creator.

DAY 183

Receive Jesus' Joy

"I have told you this so that my joy may be in you and that your joy may be complete."

John 15:11 NIV

When was the last time you experienced true, complete joy?

Jesus spoke truth into His disciples' lives so His joy would be theirs. He reminds us that joy isn't dependent on circumstances, accomplishments, or outcomes. It's found in Him, right now, right in this moment.

Too often, we postpone experiencing joy until we "arrive." When the kids are grown, when the project is finished, when the prayer is answered. Jesus invites us to experience His joy in the present moment, walking closely with Him. His complete joy becomes ours.

This kind of joy turns the mundane into meaningful and sustains us when the weight of life is heavy. Joy in Jesus is not just an expression; it's a deep gladness that no circumstance can remove.

Today, don't put off joy. Receive it. Walk in it. Let Jesus' joy overflow in you as you journey with Him.

SPEAK LIFE: "Jesus' joy is my joy, and it's complete."

TALK TO GOD: God, thank You for Jesus' joy that is also mine. Help me to receive it, live it out, and share it abundantly with others today. Amen.

REFLECT & RESPOND: What tends to entice you to delay joy until later? How can you receive Jesus' joy today, in this moment?

DAY 184

Make Time with God

"But when you pray, go away by yourself, shut the door behind you, and pray to your Father in private. Then your Father, who sees everything, will reward you."

Matthew 6:6 NLT

Does spending time with God feel like unproductive time?

In the world's eyes, time with God is not productive, but it's one of the most fruitful, life-giving habits you can grow. In a world that values visible results, God invites you away from it all to meet you and remind you that He is with you.

When you feel overwhelmed, your to-do list will always want your attention. However, choosing to spend time with God—even for a few minutes—can shift your entire perspective. It can encourage you in ways you might not expect. No perfect time-with-God routine is needed; just simple moments with your Heavenly Father satisfy and strengthen your soul.

There's no wasted time in God's presence. Time with Him is always the best answer. Those small, quiet moments with Him? They often yield the biggest breakthroughs. Why not make some time with God today?

SPEAK LIFE: "My time with God is the most important part of my day."

TALK TO GOD: Lord, remind me that time with You is never wasted. Help me to choose You before the demands of my day. Amen.

REFLECT & RESPOND: What's one simple way you can intentionally make time for God today? Ask Him for His guidance.

DAY 185

Choose Gratitude on Purpose

"And let the peace that comes from Christ rule in your hearts. For as members of one body you are called to live in peace. And always be thankful."

Colossians 3:15 NLT

Do you ever find that gratitude doesn't always happen naturally?

Sometimes it's an intentional choice to pause, notice, and give thanks, especially when life feels hurried or heavy. Paul's words remind us that thankfulness isn't just a feeling; it's a way of life.

When you choose gratitude on purpose, you're conditioning yourself to see God in your life. You begin to notice His small mercies you might otherwise miss: the kindness of a friend, the provision you didn't expect, the quiet ways God calms you.

Gratitude invites peace to rule in your heart. Where gratefulness is actively growing, worry and complaint can't survive. This is why it matters to be intentional—to make thankfulness a way of life, not just a reaction when things go well.

Today, slow down long enough to name what you're thankful for—out loud, in writing, or in prayer. An abundant life is a grateful life.

SPEAK LIFE: "I notice God in my life, and I'm grateful."

TALK TO GOD: God, lead me to live gratefully today and to make it my way of life. Amen.

REFLECT & RESPOND: What's one small thing you can thank God for right now? How can you build gratitude into the rhythms of your daily life?

DAY 186

Refuse to Believe More Is Better

> *"Those who love money will never have enough. How meaningless to think that wealth brings true happiness!"*
>
> Ecclesiastes 5:10 NLT

When have you recently believed that more will finally satisfy?

We often think "more" is better and is the answer to our longing. More money, more possessions, more opportunities, more followers. Yet, Solomon, who had more wealth and success than most, called pursuing more, meaningless. Why? Because the hunger for more never ends. Once we get what we thought would satisfy us, we quickly crave the next thing.

Chasing after more is like drinking saltwater—the more we consume, the thirstier we become. True satisfaction isn't found in acquiring, but rather in abiding and resting in God's presence and provision. More doesn't mean better; in fact, it often leads to stress, clutter, and distraction.

It's wise to ask this today: *Am I seeking fulfillment in temporary things, or am I basing my contentment in Jesus?* His peace and presence are far better than anything this world could promise.

SPEAK LIFE: "My contentment is based on Jesus, not on acquiring more."

TALK TO GOD: God, when I think more is better, remind me that stuff does not bring me happiness. Time with You does. Amen.

REFLECT & RESPOND: How are you tempted to equate "more" with satisfaction? How can you re-center your heart today on God instead?

DAY 187

Speak to Yourself As God Does

"The Spirit himself testifies with our spirit that we are God's children."

Romans 8:16 NIV

What do you say to yourself most often?

We each carry within us a soundtrack of self-talk that plays on repeat. Too often, these inner words aren't kind. They can be critical, harsh, or based on lies we've picked up somewhere. God invites us to replace this old soundtrack with something better—His truth.

Paul reminds us that the Holy Spirit testifies we are God's children. This means when you talk to yourself, you can echo His Words. Instead of, *I'll never measure up,* you can say, *I am His beloved daughter.* Instead of, *I'm a mess, and I always mess things up,* you can remind yourself, *God is patient, and He's still at work in me.*

Imagine the difference if your self-talk echoed God's voice instead of old lies. As you invite the Holy Spirit to shape your thoughts, He begins to rewrite the soundtrack of your heart. Over time, truth becomes your accompaniment, and your words evolve into a source of encouragement—not only to others, but also to yourself.

SPEAK LIFE: "I speak to myself as God speaks to me."

TALK TO GOD: God, align my self-talk today with Your truth. Amen.

REFLECT & RESPOND: What words do you need to eliminate from your self-talk? Which truths from God's Word can you use to replace them?

DAY 188

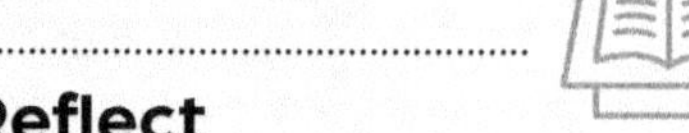

Reflect

Take a few moments to revisit the days you've just walked. There's no rush here—just honesty and grace. Feel free to journal your answers.

Reflection Prompts:

- ✓ What truth stood out to me this week?
- ✓ Where did I notice God inviting me to stop settling?
- ✓ What challenged me? What encouraged me?
- ✓ What thought/encouragement/hope do I want to carry with me into the coming days?

DAY 189

Rest

Today is a day to rest—not to catch up, fix something, or prove anything. Abundant life includes stopping long enough to receive what God is already offering you.

Sit quietly with God for a few minutes.

Breathe deeply.

Allow any Scripture from the past few days to encourage you.

Let yourself be loved and cared for by your Creator.

DAY 190

Choose Life, Not Convenience

"'Today I have given you the choice between life and death, between blessings and curses. Now I call on heaven and earth to witness the choice you make. Oh, that you would choose life, so that you and your descendants might live!"

Deuteronomy 30:19 NLT

When was the last time you had to choose between what was easy and what was life-giving?

Convenience tempts us with shortcuts, quick fixes, or decisions that feel comfortable, but they don't lead to growth. God invites us to choose life instead—what honors Him, strengthens our character, and aligns with His plans.

Choosing life often requires patience, courage, and a willingness to delay gratification. It may mean saying no to a tempting path, or staying silent when it would be easier than speaking truth. Every time we choose God's way over convenience, we invite His blessings and the abundant life He promises.

Remember, God gives you the freedom to choose, and He also gives you the strength to walk in His ways. Today, choose the path that leads to life—real, abundant, eternal life in Him.

SPEAK LIFE: "Choosing life is God's best, even if it's not convenient."

TALK TO GOD: Lord, guide me to make the choices that are life-giving, even if they aren't convenient. Amen.

REFLECT & RESPOND: Consider where convenience is tempting you to compromise. What life-giving choice can you make instead?

DAY 191

Be Eagerly Generous

"Whatever you give is acceptable if you give it eagerly. And give according to what you have, not what you don't have."

2 Corinthians 8:12 NLT

Do you ever think about *why* you give, not just *what* you give?

God isn't focused on the size of your gift, but He looks at the heart behind it. He doesn't measure generosity with a calculator, but He weighs your eagerness and sincerity. What matters is the willingness to give according to what you *have*, not what you *wish* you had.

Paul reminds us that generosity flows from God's grace. When we give eagerly, we show we trust God's provision and character. This kind of giving frees us from comparison, performance, and pressure. We do not give out of guilt or to look good. We give in response to the abundant grace we've received through Jesus.

This kind of giving delights God, and it can become an act of worship for you. No matter the amount of the gift, God calls it acceptable when it's offered with a sincere heart. Today, give eagerly out of what God has given you.

SPEAK LIFE: "God is delighted when I eagerly give to others."

TALK TO GOD: God, teach me to give eagerly out of what You've entrusted to me. Amen.

REFLECT & RESPOND: When have you recently been eagerly generous? What's one way God is calling you to do so today as an act of worship?

DAY 192

Be Strong and Courageous

"'… So be strong and courageous! Do not be afraid and do not panic before them. For the Lord your God will personally go ahead of you. He will neither fail you nor abandon you.'"

Deuteronomy 31:6 NLT

Has life felt like a battle lately?

Some days, the opposition is obvious. Other days it's subtle—the discouraging thought, the heavy burden, the unexpected setback. No matter the form the battle takes, the good news is, you don't face it alone.

God promises to be with you, to strengthen you, and to help you. He goes before you to prepare the way, and He walks with you in every step. Even when you feel surrounded or overwhelmed, the truth is you are held safely in the hands of the One Who loves you most.

Because of this, you can be strong and courageous. When you feel weak, He is strong. When you feel alone, He is near. You have everything you need for the battle with Him by your side.

SPEAK LIFE: "Even when I feel alone in the battle of life, God is always with me."

TALK TO GOD: Lord God, when life feels extra heavy, remind me that You are with me. You are all I need. Amen.

REFLECT & RESPOND: What battle in life feels overwhelming right now? How can you lean into God's presence and strength today?

DAY 193

Travel Lightly on Your Journey Home

"Dear friends, I warn you as 'temporary residents and foreigners' to keep away from worldly desires that wage war against your very souls."

1 Peter 2:11 NLT

How often do you remember this world isn't your final destination?

Peter reminds us that we are temporary residents here—pilgrims passing through on the way to a far better home. This powerful truth impacts how we live. When we know this isn't our final stop, we don't cling so tightly to possessions, accolades, or the world's approval. We travel light, keeping our hearts turned towards eternity.

As pilgrims, we are also called to live differently. Worldly desires will try to trip us up, to weigh us down, and to dull our light for Jesus. This is why Peter warns us to resist them. Our lives, though temporary here, are eternally important. How we walk, love, and shine point others to what every soul longs for: our true home.

Today, as you travel lightly through this world, keep your eyes set on your eternal home, and keep focused on impacting the lives of others along the way.

SPEAK LIFE: "I live today knowing this world is not my home."

TALK TO GOD: God, keep my attention away from the worldly distractions that pull me away from You. Amen.

REFLECT & RESPOND: What is one way you've been living for this world? How can you fix your eyes on eternity today?

DAY 194

Remember His Faithfulness

"The one who calls you is faithful, and he will do it."

1 Thessalonians 5:24 NIV

Do you ever wonder if God will really do what He says He will do?

Delays test our patience. Detours test our trust. Disappointments test our faith. Yet, Paul overrides every uncertainty with this truth: God is faithful.

This truth isn't based on your ability, your consistency, or even your courage, but instead completely on God's faithfulness. You can trust that if He called you to do something, He will equip you for it. If He has begun a work in you, He will absolutely see it through. His faithfulness guarantees it.

Faithfulness is who He is, not just what He does. He doesn't change His mind, forget His promises, or abandon His people halfway through the journey. From generation to generation, His record of faithfulness remains flawless.

This means you can take a sigh of relief today. The One Who called you will never fail you. What He has promised, He will surely bring to pass.

SPEAK LIFE: "God is faithful yesterday, today, and tomorrow."

TALK TO GOD: Heavenly Father, I praise You for Your faithfulness. Guide me to remember how faithful You are when what You've called me to do feels like too much. Amen.

REFLECT & RESPOND: What has God called you to that makes you unsure? How does His unchanging faithfulness encourage you today?

DAY 195

Reflect

Take a few moments to revisit the days you've just walked. There's no rush here—just honesty and grace. Feel free to journal your answers.

Reflection Prompts:

- ✓ What truth stood out to me this week?
- ✓ Where did I notice God inviting me to stop settling?
- ✓ What challenged me? What encouraged me?
- ✓ What thought/encouragement/hope do I want to carry with me into the coming days?

DAY 196

Rest

Today is a day to rest—not to catch up, fix something, or prove anything. Abundant life includes stopping long enough to receive what God is already offering you.

Sit quietly with God for a few minutes.

Breathe deeply.

Allow any Scripture from the past few days to encourage you.

Let yourself be loved and cared for by your Creator.

DAY 197

Walk in Your Calling

"You did not choose me, but I chose you and appointed you so that you might go and bear fruit—fruit that will last—and so that whatever you ask in my name the Father will give you."

John 15:16 NIV

Have you ever been picked last, overlooked, or ignored?

This is something hard to forget. The truth, however, is this: before you turned to Jesus, and even before you knew of His love for you, He chose you. Intentionally.

You're not here by accident or just taking up space. God appointed you for a purpose only you can fulfill. His calling on your life is deliberate and unique, and it's eternally significant. His purpose for your life proclaims that you belong to Him, and He's blessed you to be a blessing.

Chosen women live differently. Not with arrogance, but instead, with confidence. Not with pressure, but rather, with purpose. You've been chosen for His kingdom work, wherever He has you.

God didn't just save you from something. He saved you *for* something. Remember today this important truth: you are chosen, you are appointed, and you are called.

SPEAK LIFE: "God chose me on purpose for a purpose."

TALK TO GOD: Lord, guide me today to live out Your calling and to glorify You through it. Amen.

REFLECT & RESPOND: Where is God inviting you to step into your purpose today? Write a prayer of surrender and trust.

DAY 198

Lay It Down

"But with you there is forgiveness, so that we can, with reverence, serve you."

Psalm 130:4 NIV

Has lingering guilt ever plagued you?

Some guilt is like a gentle nudge of God drawing us to repentance and restoration. Lingering guilt, however, is completely different. That's the voice that replays our failures and re-accuses what God has already forgiven and forgotten.

When guilt stays too long, it distorts our view of life, God, others, and ourselves. It tricks us into believing we're still condemned, still unacceptable, still disqualified. Jesus and His sacrifice on the cross say otherwise. The Psalmist reminds us that God's forgiveness welcomes a restored relationship, reverent freedom, and a heart to serve Him.

Answer this bold question: *If God has forgiven you, who are you to withhold it from yourself?*

Refuse to carry what Jesus already took to the cross. Lay it down at His feet. Release this heavy burden you were never meant to bear. Let His mercy quiet the guilt that's overstayed its welcome. Today's the day to live free!

SPEAK LIFE: "I am free to live forgiven."

TALK TO GOD: Lord, please help me to surrender my guilt to You, accept Your forgiveness, and walk in Your love. Amen.

REFLECT & RESPOND: What guilt have you been carrying lately? What would it take today to lay it down at Jesus' feet—for good?

DAY 199

Experience His Continual Presence

"You make known to me the path of life; you will fill me with joy in your presence, with eternal pleasures at your right hand."

Psalm 16:11 NIV

Have you ever experienced the joy of being with someone who truly sees and values you?

This is just a glimpse of what it's like to live in God's presence—the One Who knows you and loves you fully. His presence isn't an occasional drop-in or a reward for good behavior. It's His continual gift to you. You don't have to clean up or work for it. You just get to be with Him—right here, right now.

On hectic days, in mundane moments, and even when life feels flipped upside-down, God's presence is always the greatest treasure. We often long for clarity, blessings, or answers, but what we actually need is Him. His presence brings joy, fullness, and peace the world can't compete with or provide.

Pause for a moment. Breathe. Smile. You are not alone. You never were, and you never will be. He is with you always.

SPEAK LIFE: "God's presence is my greatest gift."

TALK TO GOD: God, Your continual presence is reassuring. Help me to appreciate it more than anything else today. Amen.

REFLECT & RESPOND: How can you be more aware of God's presence in your everyday life? What can you do to make Him a priority today?

DAY 200

Don't Miss What's Right Here

"For everything there is a season, a time for every activity under heaven."

Ecclesiastes 3:1 NLT

Are you ever tempted to live anywhere but here?

We may rehash the past or race ahead into the future while missing what God is doing right now. We promise ourselves we'll slow down "when life settles," only to realize life never really does.

Ecclesiastes reminds us that every season—hectic or quiet, joyful or painful—has a place in God's plan. Which means this season, with all its imperfections, is significant. The moment we're in offers gifts and lessons we can't get back once they're gone.

Being present doesn't mean ignoring the future or forgetting the past. It means trusting God enough to focus on the people, work, and blessings He's placed in front of you today.

Don't let distraction or discontentment rob you of the beauty right here. God is in this very moment inviting you to notice Him, walk with Him, and delight in the life you're living now.

SPEAK LIFE: "I will stay present with God in the moments of today."

TALK TO GOD: Lord God, help me to be fully present and to look for You in every moment. Amen.

REFLECT & RESPOND: For what can you be grateful in this current season? Where do you see God in this present moment?

DAY 201

Be Grateful in the Ordinary

"So I concluded there is nothing better than to be happy and enjoy ourselves as long as we can. And people should eat and drink and enjoy the fruits of their labor, for these are gifts from God."

Ecclesiastes 3:12-13 NLT

When was the last time you were grateful for the ordinary things in your life?

We get excited about life's extraordinary moments—monumental milestones, big wins, special occasions. Yet, much of life is lived in ordinary spaces—eating a meal, completing work, talking with a friend, watching the sunset.

Scripture reminds us these everyday moments don't just take up room in our lives; they're God's gifts. God is present in life's simple rhythms, and each one welcomes opportunities for gratefulness. When we learn to see the ordinary as holy, the mundane becomes meaningful.

Practicing gratitude in the ordinary alters our perspective. We stop waiting for what's big and start noticing God's goodness right where we live.

Notice His gifts and be grateful for them today. Even if they appear to be ordinary.

SPEAK LIFE: "I am grateful in all moments, especially the ordinary ones."

TALK TO GOD: God, open my eyes to see that what may appear to be ordinary is actually a blessing from You. Amen.

REFLECT & RESPOND: What ordinary moment causes you to pause and thank God? How might you slow down enough to notice beauty every day?

DAY 202

Reflect

Take a few moments to revisit the days you've just walked. There's no rush here—just honesty and grace. Feel free to journal your answers.

Reflection Prompts:

- ✓ What truth stood out to me this week?
- ✓ Where did I notice God inviting me to stop settling?
- ✓ What challenged me? What encouraged me?
- ✓ What thought/encouragement/hope do I want to carry with me into the coming days?

DAY 203

Rest

Today is a day to rest—not to catch up, fix something, or prove anything. Abundant life includes stopping long enough to receive what God is already offering you.

Sit quietly with God for a few minutes.

Breathe deeply.

Allow any Scripture from the past few days to encourage you.

Let yourself be loved and cared for by your Creator.

DAY 204

Make the Most of Today

"Make the most of every opportunity in these evil days."

Ephesians 5:16 NLT

Are you living this season intentionally or just getting through it?

We can easily fall into the trap of simply surviving certain seasons instead of thriving in them. We tell ourselves, *After I get through this, I'll be more present.* Yet, Paul reminds us that this day and this moment are worth living on purpose, even in the fallen world in which we live.

Making the most of today is choosing to live faithfully right where you are, even if the circumstances you're in aren't easy or perfect. It's paying attention, responding with grace and wisdom, and allowing God to work through ordinary moments and unexpected situations.

You don't need a new season or wait until the next one to live meaningfully. God is already present with you in this one. This truth matters. Every day holds opportunities to love well, speak truth, extend grace, and walk with intention as you live it with God.

Don't rush past this moment. Ask God how to live wisely and fully right where He has you. This season matters.

SPEAK LIFE: "This season matters, and I am making the most of it."

TALK TO GOD: God, when I fail to live in the moment, prompt me to embrace it and look for You in it. Amen.

REFLECT & RESPOND: How have you been living just to get by lately? Write it down, and surrender it to God.

DAY 205

Choose Contentment Daily

"I am not saying this because I am in need, for I have learned to be content whatever the circumstances. I know what it is to be in need, and I know what it is to have plenty. I have learned the secret of being content in any and every situation, whether well fed or hungry, whether living in plenty or in want. I can do all this through him who gives me strength."

Philippians 4:11-13 NIV

How is God teaching you contentment in your current circumstances?

Contentment is a choice we make daily. Paul admitted contentment didn't come naturally to him; he learned it. Whether in plenty or in need, he chose to trust in Christ's strength instead of his circumstances.

We can follow his example. Each morning, before the demands begin, we can decide to live content in Jesus. It's not ignoring goals or growth, but instead refusing to let discontentment steal our joy or affect our mood.

This may look like pausing to thank God for His blessings, resisting the urge to compare, and remembering that Jesus gives you the strength to walk in contentment today. Contentment is a beautiful gift, and through Jesus, it's yours.

SPEAK LIFE: "Today, because of Jesus, I choose to walk in contentment."

TALK TO GOD: God, when discontentment rises within me, guide me to pause and be thankful. Amen.

REFLECT & RESPOND: Where do you notice discontentment creeping into your day? How could you practice gratitude right now?

DAY 206

Bless Instead of Belittle

"With the tongue we praise our Lord and Father, and with it we curse human beings, who have been made in God's likeness. Out of the same mouth come praise and cursing. My brothers and sisters, this should not be."

James 3:9-10 NIV

Have you ever praised God one moment and spoken harshly the next?

James reminds us that with the same tongue, we bless God and curse people made in His image. When we speak against others—or ourselves—we misuse this gift meant to glorify God and build up His creation.

God knit each and every one of us together with care. He considers every person His masterpiece. When we belittle ourselves, or gossip about or criticize others, we ultimately insult the Master Artist. God convicts, corrects, and guides His children, but He never condemns. If He doesn't speak words of destruction over us or others, why should we?

Speak life instead of death. Bless instead of belittle. Align your words with His truth. When you do, you live freely and help others do the same.

SPEAK LIFE: "My words are filled with life and abundance today."

TALK TO GOD: Heavenly Father, help me to use the gift of my words to speak Your truth and hope. Amen.

REFLECT & RESPOND: What words have you used to curse yourself or another lately? How can you replace them with God's truth instead?

DAY 207

Respond Generously, Not Grudgingly

"Give generously to the poor, not grudgingly, for the Lord your God will bless you in everything you do."

Deuteronomy 15:10 NLT

When you're asked to give, do you respond generously or grudgingly?

God isn't as concerned about how much you give as He is about the condition of your heart when you do. Yes, giving matters, but the attitude of your heart in the giving makes a difference. This verse isn't a command to pressure or persuade, but it's an invitation to be generous, giving from freedom instead of reluctance.

Giving grudgingly keeps score. It hesitates, fearing there won't be enough left. On the other hand, giving generously trusts the true Provider. It proceeds, affirming that what I have comes from Him, so I give because I've received.

God's blessing isn't a reward for your generosity. It begins with a heart aligned with His. You live freely when you give freely. You live abundantly when you give abundantly.

Notice today how you give. Allow it to come from gratitude, not obligation.

SPEAK LIFE: "God generously gives to me, so I generously give to others."

TALK TO GOD: Heavenly Father, when I'm asked to give, align my heart with Yours to give generously. Amen.

REFLECT & RESPOND: What are you being asked to give today? Do a heart check. Are you offering your gift generously or grudgingly? Ask God to help you.

DAY 208

Step Forward Confidently

"And God is able to bless you abundantly, so that in all things at all times, having all that you need, you will abound in every good work."

2 Corinthians 9:8 NIV

Do you ever hesitate to step into a new assignment because you don't feel quite prepared or qualified?

This is a natural response. The truth is, however, God never bases His calling on your ability alone. Instead, He fills any deficiency with His abundance. He supplies the wisdom, courage, strength, and resources you need to accomplish what He's placing before you.

He also doesn't leave you scrambling to figure it out on your own. His call is always accompanied by His provision. Who He leads, He equips.

Don't rest your confidence in your skills or your résumé. Put your confidence in God Who promises you will have all that you need to succeed in every good work. If He's called you, He will also equip you. You can freely and confidently step forward in faith with the assurance that He is already providing everything you need.

SPEAK LIFE: "God equips me for what He calls me."

TALK TO GOD: Heavenly Father, help me to remember that if You're calling me, You're already equipping me. Amen.

REFLECT & RESPOND: Where do you feel inadequate in what God is asking of you? How can you rely on His strength and provision today?

DAY 209

Reflect

Take a few moments to revisit the days you've just walked. There's no rush here—just honesty and grace. Feel free to journal your answers.

Reflection Prompts:

- ✓ What truth stood out to me this week?
- ✓ Where did I notice God inviting me to stop settling?
- ✓ What challenged me? What encouraged me?
- ✓ What thought/encouragement/hope do I want to carry with me into the coming days?

DAY 210

Rest

Today is a day to rest—not to catch up, fix something, or prove anything. Abundant life includes stopping long enough to receive what God is already offering you.

Sit quietly with God for a few minutes.

Breathe deeply.

Allow any Scripture from the past few days to encourage you.

Let yourself be loved and cared for by your Creator.

DAY 211

Set Your Mind on Things Above

"Set your minds on things above, not on earthly things."

Colossians 3:2 NIV

What is your mindset today?

It's no secret that what we think about most shapes how we live. If our minds constantly dwell on the worries, pressures, and distractions of this world, our hearts can't help but follow. Yet, Paul prods us to intentionally set our minds on things above. This is an active choice to lift our thoughts higher, beyond the temporary tug of earthly matters, and instead fix them on Jesus and His eternal kingdom.

This doesn't mean ignoring the responsibilities of daily life, but rather, aligning our thoughts with an eternal perspective. When our minds are set above, we approach our work, our relationships, and even our struggles differently. The eternal priorities of love, truth, grace, and faithfulness guide how we respond to life's everyday circumstances.

Today, fill your mind with eternal thoughts, not earthly ones. You'll live with peace, clarity, and a steady heart—no matter what comes your way.

SPEAK LIFE: "I choose to set my mind on what's above, not on earthly things."

TALK TO GOD: Lord, lead me to fill my thoughts with what's eternal, not what's earthly. Amen.

REFLECT & RESPOND: Where have your thoughts been fixed most often lately? On earthly matters or heavenly truths? How might it help you to see today's challenges through an eternal perspective?

DAY 212

Choose Words That Heal

"Gracious words are a honeycomb, sweet to the soul and healing to the bones."

Proverbs 16:24 NIV

Have your words been more stinging or soothing lately?

God reminds us that gracious words are both enjoyable and beneficial. They can bring comfort to a hurting heart, peace to an anxious mind, and strength to someone feeling weak. Oftentimes, healing begins with a single kind word.

In a world where language is often filled with harshness and criticism, Jesus is calling you to speak differently—like Him, with words that are gentle, nurturing, abundant in grace, and full of truth. Think about the last time someone lifted your spirits through what they said. Didn't it feel like a breath of fresh air? You have that same opportunity every day with the people in your life.

Ask the Lord to help you speak words of healing and hope today. Your words, filled with His love, can be the very vessel God uses to bring healing to another.

SPEAK LIFE: "My words are healing today, full of grace and love."

TALK TO GOD: Lord, equip me today to speak words full of Your grace and love. Use my words to bring healing to others. Amen.

REFLECT & RESPOND: Who in your life needs a healing word of encouragement today? How can you make this a priority every day?

DAY 213

Return to What Your Soul Needs

"My soul thirsts for God, for the living God. When can I go and meet with God?"

Psalm 42:2 NIV

What does your soul reach for when life feels full and fast?

Many things demand your attention each day—responsibilities, expectations, noises, and needs. Beneath all of it, however, your soul is quietly longing for something more, something deeper. David defines it as this: a thirst for God Himself.

This verse isn't about obligation or discipline; it's about desire. David doesn't say, "I should spend time with God." Instead, he yearns, "My soul thirsts." This kind of longing reminds us that time with God isn't meant to feel like one more task on a list. It's meant to be a time of renewal.

When your soul feels dry, distracted, or weary, it's often because it's craving connection—not productivity. God doesn't compete for your attention; He invites your heart to align with His.

Today, pause long enough to listen to your soul. Let it lead you back to the presence for which it was created.

SPEAK LIFE: "My soul thirsts for time with God."

TALK TO GOD: Lord, lead me to listen to what my soul needs, and help me to renew it by spending time with You today. Amen.

REFLECT & RESPOND: How have you tried to fill your soul with other things? How is God calling you to quench your soul's thirst for Him?

DAY 214

Ask for God's Wisdom

"If you need wisdom, ask our generous God, and he will give it to you. He will not rebuke you for asking."

James 1:5 NLT

Have you ever put off a decision because you were afraid of making the wrong one?

We may get stuck in overthinking or waiting for clarity before moving ahead. It's a good thing that God doesn't expect us to make these decisions on our own. He invites us to ask for His wisdom as we face each one.

Human wisdom may come with age, but God's wisdom is something that we cannot receive on our own. James reminds us that if we need wisdom, we can ask God for it. He will never grow tired of us asking, nor will He get upset when we do.

The next time you're facing a decision, instead of delaying it or trying to wrestle with it alone, invite God into it. Ask Him for His wisdom. Allow Him to lead you, and then rest in His faithfulness. You no longer have to do this alone.

SPEAK LIFE: "I ask for God's wisdom in every area of life."

TALK TO GOD: Lord, when I get paralyzed in making decisions, remind me to invite You in and ask for Your wisdom. Amen.

REFLECT & RESPOND: What decision are you facing today? How will you seek God's wisdom in it instead of your own?

DAY 215

Release the Backup Plan

"'But blessed is the one who trusts in the Lord, whose confidence is in him ...'"

Jeremiah 17:7 NIV

Do you trust God—but keep a backup plan just in case?

Most of us do it without even realizing it. We say we trust God, but we still try to control the outcome, manage the details, or silently believe our own plans are better. Jeremiah reminds us that blessing flows not from partial trust, but rather from placing our full confidence in the Lord.

Trusting God means letting Him be your first plan, not your emergency plan. It means believing His timing over yours, His wisdom over your knowledge, and His ways over your attempts. It's not passive; it's a bold, quiet surrender that affirms, *God, You're enough. I'm not holding onto a Plan B.*

When you make God your hope and confidence, you live differently. Pressure lessens. Fear disappears. Peace fills you. You no longer scramble to secure your future; rather, you rest in the God who already holds it.

Today, release the backup plan. Trust Him fully. Blessings begin in your surrender.

SPEAK LIFE: "God is my only plan. I trust Him fully."

TALK TO GOD: Lord, help me surrender and trust You fully today. Amen.

REFLECT & RESPOND: Have you been unintentionally clinging to a backup plan? What's one way you can begin to trust God fully instead?

DAY 216

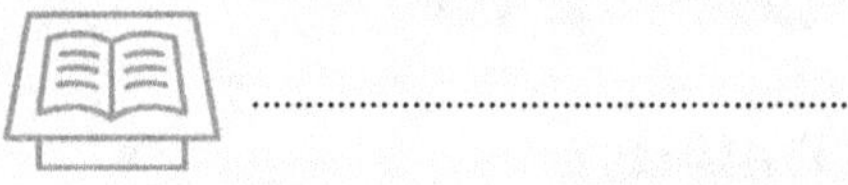

Reflect

Take a few moments to revisit the days you've just walked. There's no rush here—just honesty and grace. Feel free to journal your answers.

Reflection Prompts:

- ✓ What truth stood out to me this week?
- ✓ Where did I notice God inviting me to stop settling?
- ✓ What challenged me? What encouraged me?
- ✓ What thought/encouragement/hope do I want to carry with me into the coming days?

DAY 217

Rest

Today is a day to rest—not to catch up, fix something, or prove anything. Abundant life includes stopping long enough to receive what God is already offering you.

Sit quietly with God for a few minutes.

Breathe deeply.

Allow any Scripture from the past few days to encourage you.

Let yourself be loved and cared for by your Creator.

DAY 218

Lean into His Love

"Long ago the Lord said to Israel: 'I have loved you, my people, with an everlasting love. With unfailing love I have drawn you to myself…'"

Jeremiah 31:3 NLT

Do you ever sense God pulling you closer?

God doesn't love you from a distance. His love is always present with you. It reaches, invites, and gently draws your heart back to Him again and again. Before you ever sought Him, He was seeking you. Long before you turned toward Him, He turned His heart toward you.

His love isn't fleeting or based on your performance. It's always steady—when you feel strong in faith and when you don't. When distractions come, when doubts fill your mind, even when you drift away, His love doesn't leave. He patiently and persistently draws you back to Him.

Thankfully, you don't have to chase His love; simply embrace it. Let yourself be drawn into His presence, His peace, and His arms. There's no better place to be.

SPEAK LIFE: "God continues to draw me to Himself, and I embrace His love."

TALK TO GOD: God, thank You for Your everlasting love that never leaves. Show me how I can simply rest in it today. Amen.

REFLECT & RESPOND: How do you sense God pulling you closer to Him today? In what way will you respond to His drawing?

DAY 219

Draw Near to God

"But as for me, it is good to be near God. I have made the Sovereign Lord my refuge; I will tell of all your deeds."

Psalm 73:28 NIV

When was the last time you felt truly close to God?

Life's noise and pace can make closeness with God feel nearly impossible or something reserved for Sunday mornings. Yet, the Psalmist reminds us: being near to God is not occasional, it's a daily choice and a gift of the present.

When you draw near to God, you turn your heart toward Him in ordinary moments—folding laundry, driving to work, or sitting with a friend. It's not about doing more for Him; it's realizing He, as your Refuge, is already with you.

Drawing near to God transforms you. It shifts worry into trust, distraction into focus, and loneliness into companionship. Truly, it is good to be near God. Today, right where you are, He invites you to draw close to Him.

SPEAK LIFE: "I will draw near to God and take refuge in Him today."

TALK TO GOD: God, open my eyes to see Your presence throughout this day. Help me find security in You as my Refuge. Amen.

REFLECT & RESPOND: When during your day do you most sense God's presence? How could you intentionally draw near to Him in the ordinary moments?

DAY 220

Give Thanks Because of God's Goodness

"Give thanks to the Lord, for he is good! His faithful love endures forever."

Psalm 107:1 NLT

What would gratitude look like if it weren't tied to how you feel, but instead to Who God is?

Gratitude is more than being thankful for blessings and God's gifts; it's the natural response of a heart that is settled on God and His character. His goodness never fades or changes, and His faithful love never ends. This means you'll never run out of reasons to give God thanks.

This kind of gratitude doesn't deny difficult situations in life, but it declares God is present within them. It reminds your soul of this truth: His love, mercy, and promises all remain steady and true in your life, no matter the circumstances. When you offer gratitude that's based on God and His character, you exponentially experience the thankfulness found in God's goodness and love.

Today, let thanks permeate your thoughts and words—not just for the good you see, but also for the God Who is always good, Whose love endures forever.

SPEAK LIFE: "I am grateful because God is good. His love endures forever."

TALK TO GOD: Lord God, You are good, and I am grateful. Help me live out this gratefulness today in tangible ways. Amen.

REFLECT & RESPOND: What's one thing you can thank God for right now? How does God's goodness affect your gratitude?

DAY 221

Let God Define Healthy

"'For my thoughts are not your thoughts, neither are your ways my ways,' declares the Lord. 'As the heavens are higher than the earth, so are my ways higher than your ways and my thoughts than your thoughts ...'"

Isaiah 55:8-9 NIV

What if your definition of "healthy" looks different from God's?

We must remember, God's ways are not our ways, as Isaiah reminds us. This includes our health. According to the world, health is about a perfect body, flawless skin, or an ideal weight. God looks deeper, however. He's more concerned with your heart, wholeness, and your willingness to live aligned with Him. True health has nothing to do with culture's standards. It's about trusting your Creator, Who knows you intimately and what's best for you.

What does health look like for you today? Rest, nourishing food, movement, or laughter? Whatever it looks like, let God define healthy for you.

When you allow Him to set the standard, you'll experience peace and freedom that no diet or fitness plan could ever provide.

SPEAK LIFE: "God's definition of healthy is better than mine; He sets the standard."

TALK TO GOD: Father God, thank You for my health. Align my definition of what's healthy to Yours. Amen.

REFLECT & RESPOND: Where are you clinging to the world's definition of healthy instead of God's? What might change if you let Him define it for you?

DAY 222

Seek the Full Life

"May you experience the love of Christ, though it is too great to understand fully. Then you will be made complete with all the fullness of life and power that comes from God."

Ephesians 3:19 NLT

Where are you seeking a full life?

We often look for fullness in places such as success, approval, possessions, or even our jam-packed schedules. Yet, no matter how much we accumulate or achieve, it's never enough. The "secret" to living fully isn't really a secret at all; it's found in Jesus.

Paul's prayer reminds us that true fullness isn't something to strive for or earn; it's something Jesus came to give us. His love, His presence, and His Spirit all fill the hollow spaces within us that nothing else can fill. When we center life on Him, rest in Him, and trust Him, we live in the abundance that our circumstances cannot affect.

Living fully doesn't mean living a perfect life. It means you walk with a perfect Savior Who gives you strength, hope, and joy for every moment. This fullness lasts, and it's for you today.

SPEAK LIFE: "I live full today because my life is centered on Jesus."

TALK TO GOD: Lord, remind me that true fullness is only found in You. Amen.

REFLECT & RESPOND: Where are you tempted to seek fullness apart from God? How can you allow Him to fill you instead?

DAY 223

Reflect

Take a few moments to revisit the days you've just walked. There's no rush here—just honesty and grace. Feel free to journal your answers.

Reflection Prompts:

- ✓ What truth stood out to me this week?
- ✓ Where did I notice God inviting me to stop settling?
- ✓ What challenged me? What encouraged me?
- ✓ What thought/encouragement/hope do I want to carry with me into the coming days?

DAY 224

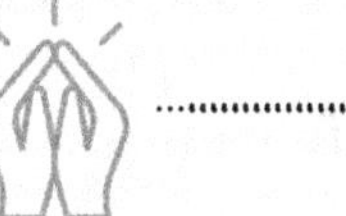

Rest

Today is a day to rest—not to catch up, fix something, or prove anything. Abundant life includes stopping long enough to receive what God is already offering you.

Sit quietly with God for a few minutes.

Breathe deeply.

Allow any Scripture from the past few days to encourage you.

Let yourself be loved and cared for by your Creator.

DAY 225

Build with Your Words

"Do not let any unwholesome talk come out of your mouths, but only what is helpful for building others up according to their needs, that it may benefit those who listen."

Ephesians 4:29 NIV

Have you considered how your words shape those around you?

Our words are powerful tools. Paul urges us to use them to build others up so that those who hear them receive grace and encouragement.

Yet, how often do we speak without thinking about the impact? A careless comment can linger in someone's heart for days—even years. Likewise, a word of encouragement, a genuine compliment, or a thoughtful note can spark hope, courage, and confidence that may never be forgotten.

Building others up with words doesn't require perfect speech. It simply requires awareness and intention. Ask God to guide your conversations, give you discernment, and highlight moments where a kind word can make a difference.

Today, choose to speak words that build, not break. Speak with love, grace, and purpose, and let your words strengthen others.

SPEAK LIFE: "My words today will encourage, bless, and bring hope to others."

TALK TO GOD: Lord, guide my words, and help me say only what's edifying to others. Amen.

REFLECT & RESPOND: Which relationship could use your uplifting words today? What's one thing you can say or text to encourage someone right now?

DAY 226

Keep Your Hands Faithful and Your Heart Humble

"I planted the seed, Apollos watered it, but God has been making it grow. So neither the one who plants nor the one who waters is anything, but only God, who makes things grow."

1 Corinthians 3:6-7 NIV

How do you feel when your efforts pay off?

When a project succeeds, or a prayer is answered, or you experience a breakthrough you've been trusting God for, you naturally feel proud, right? Paul is kind to remind us that our part in the process is obedience. God's part is to receive the glory.

We plant. We water. But only God can bring growth.

Living in this manner frees us from both pride and pressure. It's wise to remember success doesn't rest on our shoulders, and the results don't make us heroes. Every good thing points back to God, our Source for everything.

Keep your hands faithful and your heart humble. Whatever flourishes from what you do, it's all His, and He gets the glory.

SPEAK LIFE: "God brings growth, and I give Him glory."

TALK TO GOD: God, equip me daily to not take credit for the good in my life, but instead to praise You for it all. Amen.

REFLECT & RESPOND: Where are you tempted to receive glory for the results in your life? How can you redirect that praise back to God today?

DAY 227

Trust God with the Broken Pieces

"And we know that God causes everything to work together for the good of those who love God and are called according to his purpose for them."

Romans 8:28 NLT

Can you look back and see how God has used something difficult for good?

Paul isn't promising that everything in our lives *is* good. It's a promise that God works *through everything*—even what's painful, unexpected, or broken—for His ultimate good. He doesn't waste one struggle or one challenge. It's comforting to remember He weaves every single thing we go through into His greater story with care and purpose.

Sometimes, we see this clearly in hindsight. Other times, we cling to the truth that He's working behind the scenes, redeeming and restoring what we can't yet understand. Threads of both joy and sorrow are held in His capable and caring hands. He holds them all.

Today, bring your broken pieces to God. Trust Him to weave them into something beautiful for His glory and your good.

SPEAK LIFE: "I trust God is working everything out for His glory and my good."

TALK TO GOD: Lord, guide me to trust You to work everything together for good, even when life doesn't feel so good. Amen.

REFLECT & RESPOND: What in life feels difficult right now? How can you tangibly trust God to work everything out for His glory and your good?

DAY 228

Pursue Faithfulness, Not Results

"A faithful person will be richly blessed, but one eager to get rich will not go unpunished."

Proverbs 28:20 NIV

What are you pursuing and why?

This proverb contrasts two paths. One path is marked by faithfulness; it's steady obedience, integrity, and trust in God and His ways. The other is driven by eagerness; it's anxiously grasping for fortune, success, or security apart from God.

The thing about faithfulness is that it is never flashy. It doesn't cut corners or rush ahead to acquire more. It simply stays true—to God, to His ways, and to what He's entrusted to us. Scripture tells us plainly that a faithful life is the one God blesses.

The warning here isn't against God's provision; it's against pursuit fueled by misplaced desire. When gain of any kind becomes the goal, faithfulness gets compromised. Yet, when living faithfully is the goal, God's blessing follows, often in ways more meaningful than material success.

It's a good day to pause and examine what's driving your choices. Decide to choose faithfulness over fixation on results. God honors and blesses your steady, faithful heart.

SPEAK LIFE: "God calls me to live faithfully today."

TALK TO GOD: Lord, equip me to focus on living faithfully and not living for results. Guide my heart's desires today. Amen.

REFLECT & RESPOND: What are your personal pursuits lately? Write them out, then give them to God. Allow Him to mold your choices.

DAY 229

Remember He Is Close

"The Lord is close to the broken-hearted; he rescues those whose spirits are crushed."

Psalm 34:18 NLT

Have you experienced deep loss or brokenness recently?

When your heart breaks, when tears fall, when you feel all alone, God understands. The promise in Psalm 34 assures you that the Lord is close to you in your pain. He draws near to the broken-hearted, and He rescues those crushed by life's circumstances.

Notice that this verse doesn't promise the absence of hardship. We know life can bring loss, disappointment, and heartbreak. However, in the very place you feel most alone, God is often closest. His presence is a real nearness that heals, strengthens, comforts, and uplifts.

Sometimes it's in your lowest moments when you experience His love most deeply. The good news is, you never have to earn God's closeness. He's always with you. Simply turn your heart toward Him, even if all you can offer is to whisper: "Lord, I need You." You'll find He's already here.

SPEAK LIFE: "The Lord is always near, comforting and strengthening me."

TALK TO GOD: Lord, when I forget You are near me, remind me of Your comforting presence. I'm not walking this road alone. Thank You. Amen.

REFLECT & RESPOND: Where do you feel brokenhearted or crushed in spirit today? How might you invite God into that space and experience His nearness?

DAY 230

Reflect

Take a few moments to revisit the days you've just walked. There's no rush here—just honesty and grace. Feel free to journal your answers.

Reflection Prompts:

- ✓ What truth stood out to me this week?
- ✓ Where did I notice God inviting me to stop settling?
- ✓ What challenged me? What encouraged me?
- ✓ What thought/encouragement/hope do I want to carry with me into the coming days?

DAY 231

Rest

Today is a day to rest—not to catch up, fix something, or prove anything. Abundant life includes stopping long enough to receive what God is already offering you.

Sit quietly with God for a few minutes.

Breathe deeply.

Allow any Scripture from the past few days to encourage you.

Let yourself be loved and cared for by your Creator.

DAY 232

Reflect His Majesty

"So God created mankind in his own image, in the image of God he created them; male and female he created them."

Genesis 1:27 NIV

When have you doubted your uniqueness?

From the very beginning, God chose to create humans in His image—not any other of His creation, but He chose you. You bear the image of your eternal Creator. You carry His glory, beauty, creativity, and worth—not because of who you are. You bear His image because of *Whose* you are.

Yet, we forget, don't we? We twist ourselves into who we think the world wants. We chase versions of us based on comparison, not creation. However, nothing about us is random or unimportant. We reflect the God of love, power, and peace. The God who calls us good and wonderful does so because He is good and wonderful.

When you wonder and begin to doubt how special you are, return to the beginning. Return to Genesis 1. You were made in His image, and no image could be greater. Reflect His majesty today.

SPEAK LIFE: "I am made in God's image."

TALK TO GOD: God, guide me today to live in my true identity and reflect Your glory. Amen.

REFLECT & RESPOND: How does knowing you're made in God's image change how you see yourself? What part of His nature do you want to reflect more?

DAY 233

Don't Hide Your Mess

"You intended to harm me, but God intended it all for good. He brought me to this position so I could save the lives of many people."

Genesis 50:20 NLT

When you look back over your life story so far, what do you see?

Do you notice mistakes? Regrets? Chapters you'd rather skip? God sees your full story and the purpose in it. You might be embarrassed by these parts, but they are the very places where His grace shines brightest.

Joseph's life was full of betrayal, false accusations, and seasons of suffering. Yet, Joseph confidently declared, "God intended it all for good."

No part of your story is wasted in God's hands. He doesn't expect a clean, polished version of you. He uses the real, rough-around-the-edges version. The one who's been through the valleys of life. The one who continues to show up anyway.

You don't need to hide your past or minimize your journey. Your mess is the perfect setting for God's mercy and grace. Your story may encourage another in her faith today. It's never too messy to tell.

SPEAK LIFE: "God is using all of my story for good."

TALK TO GOD: God, prompt me to trust You to bring good from even the messy parts of my life. Amen.

REFLECT & RESPOND: Where do you still doubt God's redemption? How might He use it to bring hope to another?

DAY 234

Surrender to Something Better

"Then Jesus said to his disciples, 'If any of you wants to be my follower, you must give up your own way, take up your cross, and follow me. If you try to hang on to your life, you will lose it. But if you give up your life for my sake, you will save it ...'"

Matthew 16:24-25 NLT

Does surrender sound like giving up or like waving a white flag in defeat?

It may seem that way to the world, but in God's kingdom, surrender isn't weakness. It's actually power—the key to strength, freedom, and a full life.

Jesus invites us to follow Him, laying down our own will and way, and trusting He knows what's best. It's not about losing ourselves completely; it's about discovering our truest selves in Him.

What are you holding onto today that God is gently asking you to surrender? A plan, a burden, a fear, or even your desire to succeed? When you release it all to God, you gain what only He can give— peace, purpose, and the abundant life He promised.

Surrender isn't the end. It's the beautiful beginning of something better.

SPEAK LIFE: "Surrendering to God isn't weakness; it's power."

TALK TO GOD: Jesus, I trust that following You leads me to Your best for my life. Amen.

REFLECT & RESPOND: Where are you tempted to hold tightly to your own way? How can you trust Jesus with it, instead?

DAY 235

Be Faithful with Your Gifts

"His master replied, 'Well done, good and faithful servant! You have been faithful with a few things; I will put you in charge of many things. Come and share your master's happiness!'"

Matthew 25:21 NIV

What has God entrusted to you today?

Sometimes we focus on what we don't have, and we overlook what God has already gifted us. Jesus reminds us that faithfully using the gifts we've been given not only impacts others, but it also matters to God.

Perhaps God has gifted you with time, a resource, or a skill. Maybe even moments of rest. Faithfulness isn't always monumental acts; it can be simply choosing to show up, using what you have, and honoring God with it.

Being grateful for our "few things" allows us to view them as opportunities, not limitations. As we steward them well, we position ourselves to share in the joy of our Master.

Instead of waiting for a bigger platform, a larger paycheck, or a perfect time, do this: be faithful. God delights in your obedience because today's faithfulness is tomorrow's foundation.

SPEAK LIFE: "Today, I will glorify God through what He has given me."

TALK TO GOD: God, thank You for Your gifts. Guide me to steward them well and to glorify You. Amen.

REFLECT & RESPOND: What has God gifted you to use faithfully? How can you serve others and honor Him through it?

DAY 236

Offer Thanks in Jesus' Name

"And give thanks for everything to God the Father in the name of our Lord Jesus Christ."

Ephesians 5:20 NLT

When was the last time you offered thanks in Jesus' name?

Paul reminds us that the heart of gratitude is this: to give thanks for everything, to give thanks to God, and to give thanks in Jesus' name. For the woman who is filled with the Holy Spirit, this gratitude is a vital part of everyday worship and living. It honors God and reflects the love of Jesus.

Through Jesus, our gratitude has a solid, lasting foundation. We're not thankful only when God's blessings are obvious; we're thankful because we belong to Him. We're thankful because today and our future are secure in Him. Even in pain, even in heartache, even in uncertainty, we can trust His care and presence.

Offering thanks in Jesus' name is a beautiful act of faith. It declares, *I trust You, Lord, because of who You are and how You've rescued me.* It not only impacts us, but it helps others be grateful, too.

Today, let your gratitude ascend through Him—the One who makes every thanks possible.

SPEAK LIFE: "I choose gratefulness today to God through Jesus."

TALK TO GOD: God, open my heart to be grateful to You, through Jesus, for everything. Amen.

REFLECT & RESPOND: In what area is God calling you to be grateful? How will you express that gratitude today?

DAY 237

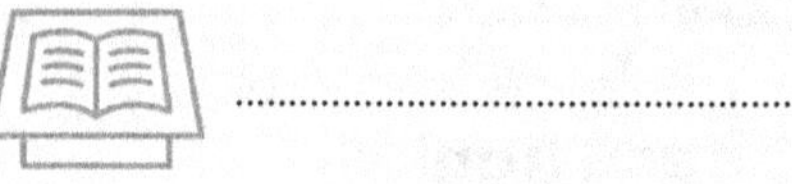

Reflect

Take a few moments to revisit the days you've just walked. There's no rush here—just honesty and grace. Feel free to journal your answers.

Reflection Prompts:

- ✓ What truth stood out to me this week?
- ✓ Where did I notice God inviting me to stop settling?
- ✓ What challenged me? What encouraged me?
- ✓ What thought/encouragement/hope do I want to carry with me into the coming days?

DAY 238

Rest

Today is a day to rest—not to catch up, fix something, or prove anything. Abundant life includes stopping long enough to receive what God is already offering you.

Sit quietly with God for a few minutes.

Breathe deeply.

Allow any Scripture from the past few days to encourage you.

Let yourself be loved and cared for by your Creator.

DAY 239

Pay Attention and Listen

"My son, pay attention to what I say; turn your ear to my words. Do not let them out of your sight, keep them within your heart; for they are life to those who find them and health to one's whole body."

Proverbs 4:20-22 NIV

What is your body telling you today—to slow down, breathe, rest, or be strengthened?

Scripture tells us the first voice to heed is God's. *Pay attention. Listen. Keep my words within your heart.* When we listen fully to God's words, we're blessed with life and health that affect our whole being. Our body's signals matter, but God's wisdom teaches us how to respond; we choose rhythms that restore, boundaries that protect, nourishment that sustains, and thoughts that align with His truth.

Keep His words close to you and within your heart. Let them guide the pace you keep, the habits you practice, and the story you speak over yourself. As you listen to God first, you'll know how to care for the body He's entrusted to you—without shame, hurry, or harshness.

Let His words be the loudest voice your body hears today.

SPEAK LIFE: "I listen and pay attention to what God is saying to me."

TALK TO GOD: Lord, help me to hear Your words today. Show me how to honor You in how I rest, nourish, and live. Amen.

REFLECT & RESPOND: What Scripture is encouraging your heart right now? How will you pause and listen for God's voice this week?

DAY 240

Recognize You Have Enough

"Then he said, 'Beware! Guard against every kind of greed. Life is not measured by how much you own.'"

Luke 12:15 NLT

Have you ever been obsessed with seeking enough?

The world entices us to strive for enough money, enough followers, enough stuff, enough success. Jesus, though, cuts straight through all this noise with His bold truth: our lives are not measured by what we own or achieve.

Remember this: enough isn't a number you'll hit someday. It's certainly not a dollar amount, a clothing size, or a hard-fought achievement. Enough is found in recognizing that Jesus is your portion and all you need. When your identity, security, and joy are centered on Him, you are free from the never-ending chase of more.

This isn't about settling for less. It's about setting your sights on truth. More won't make you more valuable. Less won't make you less loved. Enough is already yours because Jesus is yours. He is all you need.

SPEAK LIFE: "Because Jesus is enough, I already have enough."

TALK TO GOD: Lord, You are all I need. When I'm tempted to seek more in this world, remind me that no one or nothing else is enough but You. Amen.

REFLECT & RESPOND: How often do you feel tempted to measure your "enough" by numbers? How can you shift your perspective today to match Jesus'?

DAY 241

Speak God's Words

"Then the Lord reached out his hand and touched my mouth and said to me, 'I have put my words in your mouth ...'"

Jeremiah 1:9 NIV

Have you considered how God gives you words to speak?

Just as He touched Jeremiah and placed His words in his mouth, He equips you to speak into the lives of others with intention. Your words carry influence, not just for yourself, but also for those around you.

We underestimate the power of what we say. Fear, insecurity, or self-doubt may keep us quiet. Yet, God's purpose doesn't depend on our perfection; it depends on our willingness.

God gives you words to encourage the weary, redirect the wandering, or bring hope to the discouraged. He gives you the right word at the right time to change a perspective or soften a heart. He invites you to speak with courage, knowing that He has planted purpose in every word you say.

Seek God today, and ask Him to give you His words. Then, speak boldly, intentionally, and faithfully, trusting that your words carry His power.

SPEAK LIFE: "God gives me His words to speak life."

TALK TO GOD: God, help me to seek You before every conversation and to speak the words You give me. Amen.

REFLECT & RESPOND: What is God asking you to speak over yourself or someone else today? How will you respond?

DAY 242

Live Radically Generous

"Give to the one who asks you, and do not turn away from the one who wants to borrow from you."

Matthew 5:42 NIV

Do you live in such a way that people see Jesus in you?

Following Jesus is more than simply following His lead; it's to live like Him. Yet, the ways of Jesus often look radical compared to the ways of the world. While the world encourages us to keep what we've earned, Jesus spurs us on to give abundantly to those who ask.

This kind of generosity is also radical, and it involves all areas of our lives. It's being so sold out for Jesus, that we give like He gives, we love like He loves, and we bless others like He does. It's living in such a way that people see Him in us.

Yes, radical generosity can make us feel uncomfortable. It might even seem costly. Giving really isn't about us at all, though. It's about the One we represent. The One Who gave everything for us. Giving is all about Jesus. When we live generously, we show the world what Jesus looks like.

SPEAK LIFE: "Because I live for Jesus, I am radically generous."

TALK TO GOD: Lord, guide me to give like You give, to love as You love, and to bless others as You do. Amen.

REFLECT & RESPOND: Where is God calling you to be more generous? How can you emulate Jesus' example of radical generosity today?

DAY 243

Patiently Endure Testing and Temptation

"God blesses those who patiently endure testing and temptation. Afterward they will receive the crown of life that God has promised to those who love him."

James 1:12 NLT

Are you experiencing a trial right now?

Life can be full of them. We encounter temptations, hardships, and disappointments, yet God calls us to endure them patiently. Every trial faced with faith is shaping us, strengthening us, and preparing us for what's ahead.

James points us to this promise that lifts our perspective: the crown of life. This crown is not a fading trophy or a temporary reward. It is eternal life with God, the fulfillment of all His promises, and the joy of His presence forever. We can't earn it; it's freely given to those who love Jesus and follow Him.

When present trials feel heavy and overwhelming, you have hope in this promise. Walk steadfastly, with your eyes fixed on this eternal reward. The crown of life awaits you—and friend, it will be worth it all.

SPEAK LIFE: "I remain steadfast; God's crown of life is waiting for me."

TALK TO GOD: Heavenly Father, when life feels heavy with trials, lift my perspective and remind me of the crown of life that awaits me. Amen.

REFLECT & RESPOND: What trial are you currently enduring? How does the promise of the crown of life encourage you to stay faithful today?

DAY 244

Reflect

Take a few moments to revisit the days you've just walked. There's no rush here—just honesty and grace. Feel free to journal your answers.

Reflection Prompts:

- ✓ What truth stood out to me this week?
- ✓ Where did I notice God inviting me to stop settling?
- ✓ What challenged me? What encouraged me?
- ✓ What thought/encouragement/hope do I want to carry with me into the coming days?

DAY 245

Rest

Today is a day to rest—not to catch up, fix something, or prove anything. Abundant life includes stopping long enough to receive what God is already offering you.

Sit quietly with God for a few minutes.

Breathe deeply.

Allow any Scripture from the past few days to encourage you.

Let yourself be loved and cared for by your Creator.

DAY 246

Rest Under His Wings

"He will cover you with his feathers. He will shelter you with his wings. His faithful promises are your armor and protection."

Psalm 91:4 NLT

When life feels overwhelming, where do you run?

The world feels loud, heavy, and uncertain some days. Fear creeps in, and peace becomes nonexistent. In these moments, God invites you to draw close to Him—not to do anything, but rather to simply rest under His covering, in His shelter. You don't have to come strong or composed; you only have to come. He is near, and His refuge is not reserved for the put-together ones; it is a sanctuary for the weary and worn.

This paints for us a beautiful picture of a protective Father, pulling His children close, shielding them with strength and tenderness. His faithfulness surrounds us like armor. His presence is our refuge. He has us safe, secure, and sheltered.

You aren't standing exposed or fighting alone. You no longer have to hold yourself up or together. Let your Father's faithfulness cover what feels fragile and overwhelming. Rest under His wings today. You are safe, seen, and lovingly held in His arms.

SPEAK LIFE: "I rest in God's loving care today."

TALK TO GOD: Heavenly Father, when I feel overwhelmed, prompt me to come to You and rest in Your care and safety. Amen.

REFLECT & RESPOND: What feels overwhelming in life right now? How can you tangibly rest in God's care today?

DAY 247

Step Into Your Fresh Start

"This means that anyone who belongs to Christ has become a new person. The old life is gone; a new life has begun!"

2 Corinthians 5:17 NLT

Do you ever believe that you are a combination of your past mistakes, miscalculations, or missed opportunities?

Paul offers a fresh perspective. In Jesus, you are not only free and forgiven—you are made *new*. Not patched up. Not slightly improved. You are completely and beautifully new. Let that sink in.

Redemption is God's specialty. He takes what the world calls ruined and rubbish, and He reclaims it for His glory. He doesn't just erase your past, He rewrites your future. The shame that once defined you? Gone. The regret that weighed heavily for years? Lifted.

This is your fresh start. Right now. It's here waiting for you. You don't have to keep proving you've changed or questioning that you deserve it. God's grace has already done the work. Your job is simply to walk into it.

You've been redeemed and reclaimed by the One Who makes all things new—including you.

SPEAK LIFE: "My past no longer defines me—God does."

TALK TO GOD: Lord, Help me to walk in this newness of life, letting go of the past, and trusting You with the future. Amen.

REFLECT & RESPOND: Where do you still carry the weight of your past? How can you embrace Jesus' freedom instead?

DAY 248

Take Heart in the Ashes

"To all who mourn in Israel, he will give a crown of beauty for ashes, a joyous blessing instead of mourning, festive praise instead of despair. In their righteousness, they will be like great oaks that the Lord has planted for his own glory."

Isaiah 61:3 NLT

Is pain like a layer of soot on your soul?

Maybe you're still feeling the sting of all you've walked through as traces of heartbreak, failure, or loss remain. Thankfully, God never leaves His daughters in the ashes. He steps in with compassion and redemption.

Isaiah declares that God can transform anything. That deep pain? He can heal it. That broken dream? He can repurpose it. That chapter you wish to erase? He can bring beauty from it.

God trades sorrow for joy, despair for praise, and brokenness for hope. He doesn't just sweep away the past, He reshapes it into something holy and beautiful.

If you find yourself in the ashes today, take heart! Your story isn't over. Your ashes aren't wasted. God can use them as the very ingredients for goodness in your life—and all for His glory.

SPEAK LIFE: "God brings beauty from my past."

TALK TO GOD: God, lead me to trust that You are bringing beauty from the ashes of my life. Amen.

REFLECT & RESPOND: What ashes in your life can you invite God to transform? What beauty has He already brought from past pain?

DAY 249

Live Courageously While Facing Fear

"'… For if you remain silent at this time, relief and deliverance for the Jews will arise from another place, but you and your father's family will perish. And who knows but that you have come to your royal position for such a time as this?'"

Esther 4:14 NIV

How courageous are you living today?

Living courageously is choosing obedience, even while facing fear. Esther knew the risk of approaching the king without being summoned; it could cost her life. Yet, Mordecai's words prompted her to see beyond her fear. God had placed her there, not for comfort or safety, but rather for impact.

We face moments like this, too. Maybe it's speaking truth in love, standing firm in our faith, or stepping into an assignment we'd rather avoid. When we remember Who is with us, we can live courageously.

Be courageous today, because fear has no hold on you. The size of your courage doesn't determine the outcome. The size of your God does. Trust the One Who has placed you here "for such a time as this."

SPEAK LIFE: "I will choose to live courageously today."

TALK TO GOD: God, help me be courageous in the face of fear. Strengthen me, encourage me, and help me be brave in You. Amen.

REFLECT & RESPOND: Where is God calling you to step out bravely right now? How will you trust Him in this today?

DAY 250

Let Go and Live Free

"No, dear brothers and sisters, I have not achieved it, but I focus on this one thing: Forgetting the past and looking forward to what lies ahead, I press on to reach the end of the race and receive the heavenly prize for which God, through Christ Jesus, is calling us."

Philippians 3:13-14 NLT

Does letting go ever feel risky?

What if I get hurt again? What if I'm not ready? Holding on to what's behind us—old wounds, past versions of ourselves, mistakes, missed opportunities—keeps us from stepping into the abundance God has for us right now.

Paul knew this. He lived it. His past could have disqualified him, but he didn't let it define him. Instead, he pressed forward, focusing on the prize ahead: Jesus.

Letting go is releasing the burdensome weight of the past so we can live light and run free today. It's choosing hope over regret and purpose over pain. It's trusting that God is doing something new ahead, even if we can't yet see it.

Don't stay stuck in a chapter God has already finished. Let go and live free.

SPEAK LIFE: "I live free today by letting go of the past."

TALK TO GOD: God, guide me to release my past to live in Your freedom today. Amen.

REFLECT & RESPOND: What is God inviting you to release? How would your life feel lighter if you did?

DAY 251

Reflect

Take a few moments to revisit the days you've just walked. There's no rush here—just honesty and grace. Feel free to journal your answers.

Reflection Prompts:

- ✓ What truth stood out to me this week?
- ✓ Where did I notice God inviting me to stop settling?
- ✓ What challenged me? What encouraged me?
- ✓ What thought/encouragement/hope do I want to carry with me into the coming days?

DAY 252

Rest

Today is a day to rest—not to catch up, fix something, or prove anything. Abundant life includes stopping long enough to receive what God is already offering you.

Sit quietly with God for a few minutes.

Breathe deeply.

Allow any Scripture from the past few days to encourage you.

Let yourself be loved and cared for by your Creator.

DAY 253

Be Trustworthy in the Little Things

"'Whoever can be trusted with very little can also be trusted with much, and whoever is dishonest with very little will also be dishonest with much...'"

Luke 16:10 NIV

Do you ever underestimate the value of what's small?

Our unseen acts of obedience can appear insignificant—folding the laundry, showing up on time, doing the tasks we've put off, or encouraging a friend. Yet, these are not insignificant to God.

The little things matter, and Jesus teaches that being trustworthy in them is the training ground for greater responsibility. It's in these moments, when no one is watching, that we become transformed. Every small, trustworthy act builds a life of integrity and faithfulness.

If you've been longing for a bigger assignment, remember: God often measures readiness by how we handle what He's already given us. Your patient consistency today might be the very thing preparing you for tomorrow's calling.

Don't despise what's small or what feels ordinary. God is growing you through it, and in His kingdom, your trustworthiness will not be wasted.

SPEAK LIFE: "I am trustworthy with what God has given me."

TALK TO GOD: Lord God, equip me daily to be trustworthy in the little things. Amen.

REFLECT & RESPOND: Where is God asking you to be consistent right now? How might that trustworthiness be preparing you for more?

DAY 254

Accept God's Compassion

"But you, Lord, are a compassionate and gracious God, slow to anger, abounding in love and faithfulness."

Psalm 86:15 NIV

Do you ever doubt God's compassion toward you?

God doesn't walk away. Especially on the days we feel like we've failed. Perhaps we've snapped in frustration, neglected prayer, or entertained unhealthy thoughts or actions. God is present. He shows up with compassion and grace. Always. Do we show ourselves that same compassion and grace?

God isn't with us only on our good days, and thankfully, our worth doesn't change because of our choices or our feelings. God looks at us with love and is always faithful, even when we aren't. On our worst days, we are still loved, still chosen, and still God's beloved daughters. Let this truth sink in today.

When you fall short, don't allow yourself to spiral into shame or regret. Instead, accept God's compassion and permit it to fill you. Let His grace pick you up, dust you off, and remind you that you are His beloved.

SPEAK LIFE: "Even on off days, God still shows me compassion."

TALK TO GOD: Lord, help me remember that Your love, compassion, and grace aren't a result of what I do, but rather of Who You are. Amen.

REFLECT & RESPOND: How does God's compassion toward you change the way you see yourself? What can you do to accept His compassion today?

DAY 255

Don't Let Comparison Rob You

"Pay careful attention to your own work, for then you will get the satisfaction of a job well done, and you won't need to compare yourself to anyone else. For we are each responsible for our own conduct."

Galatians 6:4-5 NLT

Could comparison be stealing your contentment?

Comparison is a subtle thief. It sneaks in, whispering lies that someone else is prettier, holier, more successful, or simply better than you. Before you realize it, it's robbed you of joy, and your contentment has vanished.

Paul is reminding you to stay focused on your own calling, work, and walk with God. When your eyes are on someone else's space, you miss the beauty in your own. God didn't design you to live her story; He designed you to live yours.

Your value isn't based on anyone else but Jesus. He settled your worth at the cross. If comparison is stealing your contentment, today is the day to lay it down. Go to Jesus and embrace the beautiful, abundant life He designed for you.

SPEAK LIFE: "My value and contentment are in Jesus alone."

TALK TO GOD: Lord God, when I'm tempted to compare my life to others, remind me that I already have Your best. Amen.

REFLECT & RESPOND: In what areas are you most tempted to compare yourself? How might God be inviting you to shift from comparison to contentment today?

DAY 256

Show Up and Dispel Darkness

"Feed the hungry, and help those in trouble. Then your light will shine out from the darkness, and the darkness around you will be as bright as noon."

Isaiah 58:10 NLT

When was the last time you showed up for someone in need?

Isaiah reminds us that when we meet the practical needs of others—feeding the hungry, helping those in trouble—light breaks into the darkness. When we intentionally show up for others, a spark of hope ignites in someone else's story. What may feel like a small gesture to us may be the very answer to someone else's desperate prayer.

Think about Jesus for a moment. He intentionally showed up for others His entire life. He served the broken, offered hope to the lost, and endured the cross for us all. Still today, His sacrifice offers the gift of salvation to all who believe.

Don't underestimate the power of showing up. Your willingness to love, give, or serve enables another to experience the presence of Jesus. When that happens, darkness doesn't stand a chance.

SPEAK LIFE: "When I show up for another, Jesus shines through me."

TALK TO GOD: Lord God, remind me that showing up for others doesn't just impact them, but it also dispels darkness in this world. Amen.

REFLECT & RESPOND: For whom is God calling you to show up today? What step will you take to do that?

DAY 257

Replace Complaining with Blessing

"Do everything without complaining and arguing, so that no one can criticize you. Live clean, innocent lives as children of God, shining like bright lights in a world full of crooked and perverse people."

Philippians 2:14-15 NLT

What do you complain about most often?

Whether it's about our circumstances, the weather, others, or even ourselves, we can easily slip into complaining. Yet, God calls us to a higher way—one that lives without grumbling and shines brightly in a world fixated on what's wrong.

Complaining drains our energy and clouds our perspective. On the other hand, blessing carries unmistakable power; it encourages, strengthens, and can even shift situations in unexpected ways. By speaking blessings over our circumstances, our families, and our friends, we become a part of God's transformational work—one that's full of gratitude, faith, and hope.

Today, pay attention to your words. Replace complaining with blessing, and grumbling with God's goodness. Even small, intentional words of blessing can turn a complaining habit into a heart of gratitude and joy.

SPEAK LIFE: "I speak words of blessing over me, my family, and friends."

TALK TO GOD: God, help me to do everything without complaining and to speak Your words of blessing instead. Amen.

REFLECT & RESPOND: How can you intentionally speak blessing into your circumstances today? In what area will you choose to bless and not complain?

DAY 258

Reflect

Take a few moments to revisit the days you've just walked. There's no rush here—just honesty and grace. Feel free to journal your answers.

Reflection Prompts:

- ✓ What truth stood out to me this week?
- ✓ Where did I notice God inviting me to stop settling?
- ✓ What challenged me? What encouraged me?
- ✓ What thought/encouragement/hope do I want to carry with me into the coming days?

DAY 259

Rest

Today is a day to rest—not to catch up, fix something, or prove anything. Abundant life includes stopping long enough to receive what God is already offering you.

Sit quietly with God for a few minutes.

Breathe deeply.

Allow any Scripture from the past few days to encourage you.

Let yourself be loved and cared for by your Creator.

DAY 260

Don't Look Back

"Jesus replied, 'No one who puts a hand to the plow and looks back is fit for service in the kingdom of God.'"

Luke 9:62 NIV

In what direction are you looking—forward or backward?

A farmer plowing a field must keep his eyes facing forward. If he looks back, the rows become crooked. In the same way, when we focus on the past—our regrets, mistakes, or even former joys—we lose sight of the life God is calling us to right now.

Jesus reminds us that looking back is not His best. It often keeps us stuck. Maybe it's pondering second guesses, clinging to old habits, or wishing for how things used to be. Jesus' plans for us today are too important to be hindered by yesterday.

Moving forward isn't forgetting your past; it's refusing to let it control your present. God redeems what's behind you and equips you for what's ahead. Your calling is forward-facing and full of His hope, purpose, and promises.

Today, keep your hand steady on the plow. Fix your eyes on Jesus. The best is not behind you. It's before you.

SPEAK LIFE: "Instead of looking back, I stay present with Jesus."

TALK TO GOD: God, equip me to keep my eyes straight ahead on You today. My past is over. Amen.

REFLECT & RESPOND: What is causing you to glance backwards? How can you take a step forward instead?

DAY 261

Hold On Through Suffering

"Yet what we suffer now is nothing compared to the glory he will reveal to us later."

Romans 8:18 NLT

Are you facing struggles or pain today?

We live in a broken world, so it's no wonder we experience brokenness in it. Pain, loss, and difficulty affect us in various ways. Yet, Paul reminds us that no matter what we face here, it's nothing compared to the joy awaiting us in God's presence.

Our suffering here is temporary, while the joy of eternity is forever. The glory of heaven will far surpass the heaviness of today's trials. This truth strengthens us to endure our struggles with patience and hope. When we shift our focus from what is hurting now to what is promised, joy seeps into the cracks of our suffering. This may not erase the pain, but it gives it purpose and reminds us that it's not the end of the story.

Today, hold on with patient joy. Keep your eyes lifted. What awaits you will be more beautiful and glorious than you can imagine.

SPEAK LIFE: "Today's struggles can't compare to the glory ahead."

TALK TO GOD: God, when today's sufferings feel overwhelming, point me to Your truth, confirming that what's to come outweighs the difficulties now. Amen.

REFLECT & RESPOND: What current hardship feels heavy right now? Write it down, and ask God to help you endure it with patience and hope.

DAY 262

Please God with Your Faith

"And without faith it is impossible to please God, because anyone who comes to him must believe that he exists and that he rewards those who earnestly seek him."

Hebrews 11:6 NIV

Are you living out a faith that pleases God?

This verse speaks this clear truth: faith is essential to your walk with God. Without it, pleasing Him isn't possible.

Faith is not hopeful wishing or positive thinking. It's also not pretending everything is fine or ignoring what's real. Faith is choosing to trust God in the middle of real life. It is believing His character is unchanging, His promises are true, and His presence is near, even when circumstances look questionable.

Faith is showing up with your questions and weaknesses and still saying, "Lord, I trust You." It's not a one-time event. Instead, it's a daily, sometimes moment-by-moment, choice to rely on God instead of yourself, to believe His way is better, and to keep seeking Him.

This kind of faith delights God. It shows you truly believe that He is who He says He is.

SPEAK LIFE: "My faith shows I believe God is who He says He is."

TALK TO GOD: Lord, please guide me today to please You through my faith. Help me rely on You and share You with others. Amen.

REFLECT & RESPOND: What misconceptions about faith have you held onto? How can you practice real, grounded faith in God today?

DAY 263

Believe Truth, Not Shame

"Those who look to him are radiant; their faces are never covered with shame."

Psalm 34:5 NIV

Have you recently heard shame whispering lies about you?

Shame is nothing but a liar. It belittles, destroys, and insists your past defines you, your failures disqualify you, and you'll never measure up—no matter how hard you try. Thankfully, God says otherwise.

You are not your past mistakes. You are not what was done to you or what you regret. You are redeemed, made new, and wholly loved by God. His presence overrides every one of shame's lies.

Shame says hide. Jesus says come close. Shame says stay stuck. Jesus says you're free. When you look to Jesus and believe His truth, your life begins to shine. You walk taller. You live lighter. You know without a doubt that He is living in You and through You.

Today, allow shame to fall defeated at the feet of Jesus—the One Who laid down His life for you and Who loves you most. Shame has no claim on a daughter of the King.

SPEAK LIFE: "God and His love have freed me from shame."

TALK TO GOD: Lord, continue to remind me I'm Your daughter—free, full of hope, and blessed by You. Amen.

REFLECT & RESPOND: Where has shame shown up in your life? What's one way you can replace shame's lies with His love today?

DAY 264

Be Thankful as an Act of Faith

"One of them, when he saw he was healed, came back, praising God in a loud voice. He threw himself at Jesus' feet and thanked him—and he was a Samaritan. Jesus asked, 'Were not all ten cleansed? Where are the other nine? Has no one returned to give praise to God except this foreigner?' Then he said to him, 'Rise and go; your faith has made you well.'"

Luke 17:15-19 NIV

When has gratitude deepened your trust in God?

Luke shares how ten lepers were healed, but only one returned to thank and praise Jesus. He heard Jesus proclaim how his faith made him well.

This man's gratitude was an act of faith. By coming back to Jesus and acknowledging the source of his healing, he trusted Him for more. His thankfulness recognized Jesus' authority, goodness, and worthiness to be praised.

Gratitude strengthens our faith, too. Each time we thank God, we recognize the history of His faithfulness. Our trust deepens, and our faith increases.

The more we thank Him for what He's done, the more confident we become in what He will do.

SPEAK LIFE: "I thank God for all He's done and for all He'll do."

TALK TO GOD: God, help me remember how giving You thanks grows my faith in You. Amen.

REFLECT & RESPOND: When has God shown His faithfulness to you recently? How will you thank Him today?

DAY 265

Reflect

Take a few moments to revisit the days you've just walked. There's no rush here—just honesty and grace. Feel free to journal your answers.

Reflection Prompts:

- ✓ What truth stood out to me this week?
- ✓ Where did I notice God inviting me to stop settling?
- ✓ What challenged me? What encouraged me?
- ✓ What thought/encouragement/hope do I want to carry with me into the coming days?

DAY 266

Rest

Today is a day to rest—not to catch up, fix something, or prove anything. Abundant life includes stopping long enough to receive what God is already offering you.

Sit quietly with God for a few minutes.

Breathe deeply.

Allow any Scripture from the past few days to encourage you.

Let yourself be loved and cared for by your Creator.

DAY 267

Recognize He's Close

Does God ever seem far away?

Maybe you think your prayers are unheard, and your soul feels dry from the silence. Perhaps you open your Bible, but the words seem distant or dull. You wonder, *Is God really as near as He promises?*

Our feelings don't always tell the truth, but God always does. He is continually near. Not just theoretically or theologically, but also personally, presently, and intimately. He is not waiting for us to do anything on our end. He's already with us—ready, willing, and available.

King David reminds us that God draws close to those who call on Him. Not with perfect prayers or flawless faith, but He shows up through our honest words and open hearts.

When you whisper a weary prayer, He hears. When the world screams you are unseen, He sees. When you're lonely, He's closer than your next breath. You don't have to chase Him down or earn His presence. You already have it. You already have Him. Right now. Right here. He is near.

SPEAK LIFE: "God is closer than my next breath."

TALK TO GOD: God, help me remember You are always with me, constantly and trustworthily. Amen.

REFLECT & RESPOND: What causes you to feel distant from God? How can you call on Him in truth today?

DAY 268

Surrender and Be Strengthened

"Then Jesus said, 'Come to me, all of you who are weary and carry heavy burdens, and I will give you rest. Take my yoke upon you. Let me teach you, because I am humble and gentle at heart, and you will find rest for your souls. For my yoke is easy to bear, and the burden I give you is light.'"

Matthew 11:28-30 NLT

Are you weary and burdened?

The world encourages us to push through, try harder, and carry life's burdens ourselves. Jesus offers a different way—one that begins with giving to Him the things draining us.

This is surrender. It's knowing we weren't created to bear the weight of life alone. When we release our burdens into His hands, we don't just lighten our load, but we also gain His strength.

Jesus reminds us His yoke allows a shared load. He walks alongside us, steadying our steps and supplying every need for our journey. True rest for our souls is found in trusting Him enough to carry what we cannot.

If you're weary and burdened today, surrender what's draining you, and find the strength for which you're longing.

SPEAK LIFE: "Jesus gives me rest as I surrender my burdens."

TALK TO GOD: Jesus, help me to surrender my life and its burdens to You. Amen.

REFLECT & RESPOND: What's one burden you can entrust to Jesus today? How will you encourage another to do the same?

DAY 269

Be Wise and Lift Your Eyes

"Be wise in the way you act toward outsiders; make the most of every opportunity."

Colossians 4:5 NIV

How often do we miss opportunities because we're rushing through life with our heads down?

Paul's reminder calls us to walk wisely, especially in the way we interact with those who don't yet know Jesus.

This wisdom isn't about long dialogues or big gestures. It's about small, Spirit-led moments, such as stopping to listen, offering kindness, or showing grace when it's easier to act otherwise. God often opens doors in our everyday interactions at just the right time. Whether it's a conversation in the checkout line, a wave for a weary neighbor, or an encouraging word for a grieving friend.

When we lift our eyes, we start to see our days are filled with amazing, God-ordained opportunities. These aren't interruptions. They are beautiful invitations.

Today, slow down enough to notice. Your presence, your words, and your actions may be the glimpse of Jesus someone else needs.

SPEAK LIFE: "I notice others and use God's wisdom in my interactions with them."

TALK TO GOD: God, lift my eyes to see who You've placed in my path. Give me Your wisdom in how to bless them. Amen.

REFLECT & RESPOND: How can you intentionally slow down to notice others today? What's one way you can impact their lives for good?

DAY 270

Do It with Thanks

"And whatever you do, whether in word or deed, do it all in the name of the Lord Jesus, giving thanks to God the Father through him."

Colossians 3:17 NIV

How different would life look if gratitude affected every word and action?

Paul, here, encourages us who follow Jesus to live out our faith in our everyday kind of moments. Gratitude is the manner in which we carry this out. Thankfulness reminds us Who we belong to, Who we represent, and Who empowers us to love others well.

When you give thanks in every word or action, you're inviting God into your ordinary moments. Making the bed, sending an email, running errands—these daily tasks can all become expressions of gratitude and worship when offered in Jesus' name. Gratitude shifts your heart from routine to reverence, from obligation to opportunity.

Living this way means you choose to acknowledge God's goodness in all things. As you do, your words and actions become a testimony of His presence in your everyday life.

SPEAK LIFE: "My faith in Jesus causes me to be thankful in all of life."

TALK TO GOD: God, show me where I've not been grateful lately, and change my heart as a result. Amen.

REFLECT & RESPOND: What is one way God is calling you to be grateful today? How could doing so be a testimony to others?

DAY 271

Release the Idol of Control

Have you ever thought about how control can quietly take God's place in our hearts?

It can become the thing we cling to when life feels uncertain or overwhelming. We may try to handle every outcome, micromanage relationships, and hold our plans tightly, all in an effort to feel "safe." Idolatry isn't just about statues and sins; it can be subtle, like with the need to control.

When control takes over, it blocks the peace, power, and freedom God longs to give. We become burdened, weary, and disconnected from the very One Who wants to lead us to His best.

The good news? God invites us to release this idol and trade it for His trust and rest. When we surrender control, we find true freedom from the weight of idol worship and from carrying burdens not meant for us.

Today, choose to turn from control and give God His rightful place. There you'll find His perfect peace and rest.

SPEAK LIFE: "I release my need to control and trust God instead."

TALK TO GOD: God, show me where control has become an idol in my life. Help me tear it down. Amen.

REFLECT & RESPOND: What areas of your life feel most difficult to give up control? How can you release that control to God today?

DAY 272

Reflect

Take a few moments to revisit the days you've just walked. There's no rush here—just honesty and grace. Feel free to journal your answers.

Reflection Prompts:

- ✓ What truth stood out to me this week?
- ✓ Where did I notice God inviting me to stop settling?
- ✓ What challenged me? What encouraged me?
- ✓ What thought/encouragement/hope do I want to carry with me into the coming days?

DAY 273

Rest

Today is a day to rest—not to catch up, fix something, or prove anything. Abundant life includes stopping long enough to receive what God is already offering you.

Sit quietly with God for a few minutes.

Breathe deeply.

Allow any Scripture from the past few days to encourage you.

Let yourself be loved and cared for by your Creator.

DAY 274

Live Abundantly Filled

"The Lord is my shepherd; I have all that I need. He lets me rest in green meadows; he leads me beside peaceful streams. He renews my strength. He guides me along right paths, bringing honor to his name."

Psalm 23:1-3 NLT

How often are you running on empty?

Somewhere along the way, we've bought into the lie that running on empty is normal. We cram our schedules, push beyond exhaustion, and ignore the warning signs of our bodies and souls. Yet, God never intended for His daughters to live this way.

Psalm 23 is a gentle reminder that the Lord, our Shepherd, leads us to rest, renewal, and the right paths for our lives. No amount of striving, hustling, or powering through can match God's rhythms of quiet, stillness, and restoration. Just as a car can't keep going without fuel, we can't keep pouring out without being filled again by Him.

If you're weary, you're not failing; you're human. God delights in renewing your strength. He alone is your Source. You're not meant to run on empty. You're meant to live abundantly filled by your Shepherd

SPEAK LIFE: "I rest in God, trusting Him to renew my strength."

TALK TO GOD: God, prompt me to rest in You before I become weary and exhausted. Amen.

REFLECT & RESPOND: Where do you feel most empty right now? How can you allow your Shepherd to restore you?

DAY 275

Be Grateful for Who He Is

"Give thanks to the Lord, for he is good. His love endures forever."

Psalm 136:1 NIV

What if your gratefulness didn't depend on your circumstances?

Psalm 136 begins with this simple and profound truth: God is good, and His love endures forever. This means His goodness is always constant and consistent, even when our circumstances or situations aren't. His love is always unconditional and unwavering, even when ours is not.

Our gratefulness is often tied to good outcomes. Yet, Scripture invites us to a deeper kind of gratitude—one based on Who God is, not on our circumstances. When we center our thoughts on God's goodness and love, no matter what is happening around us, we become increasingly thankful for His presence and provision.

Grateful daughters live differently. We appreciate what others miss, we see through perspectives others don't, and we notice the good amidst trying times.

When your circumstances are challenging, and your gratitude wears thin, remember God's goodness and enduring love. Doing so will lead you to His abundance.

SPEAK LIFE: "God's goodness and love fill my heart with gratefulness."

TALK TO GOD: Lord, help me remember Your goodness and love when my gratefulness wears thin. Amen.

REFLECT & RESPOND: How has God and His goodness blessed you recently? In what way will you show your gratitude to Him today?

DAY 276

Embrace the Strength of Silence

"The one who has knowledge uses words with restraint, and whoever has understanding is even-tempered. Even fools are thought wise if they keep silent, and discerning if they hold their tongues."

Proverbs 17:27-28 NIV

Does silence ever feel like weakness to you?

This world rewards fast responses and loud opinions, and silence often appears as a deficiency. Yet, Solomon reveals this opposite truth: silence is often an indication of wisdom and strength.

Sometimes the most powerful response may be no response at all. Silence gives space for God to work in ways that our words cannot. It often allows tempers to cool, hearts to soften, and perspectives to shift. Silence can also be an act of humility that signals choosing to listen instead of insisting to being heard.

Choosing silence discerns when your words may add value and when they might make matters worse. Today, consider where silence might be your strongest statement. By holding back unnecessary words, you invite peace, understanding, and the presence of God into the moment.

SPEAK LIFE: "I trust God to guide me when to speak and when to stay silent."

TALK TO GOD: Lord God, lead me in all situations to speak or to stay silent. You know what's best. Amen.

REFLECT & RESPOND: When has God used your silence for good in the past? In what situation today would your silence speak louder than words?

DAY 277

....

Bless in Secret

"But when you give to someone in need, don't let your left hand know what your right hand is doing. Give your gifts in private, and your Father, who sees everything, will reward you."

Matthew 6:3-4 NLT

Have you ever blessed someone in secret?

The world's generosity is showy, recognition-driven, and praise-seeking. Jesus calls us to give generously in another way—in private—where God is the only one who sees and Who will reward our giving.

Blessing in secret, shifts our focus from human approval to godly blessing. It has nothing to do with expectation, the size of the gift, or receiving acknowledgment. It's all about the joy and blessing God pours into our act of giving.

When we bless quietly, we also acknowledge the sacredness of the gift. We honor both the person receiving it and the One who provides it. Secret generosity trains our hearts to delight in God's approval above all else. It reminds us that God will use our gift in ways we cannot yet see—both in the recipient's life and in ours.

SPEAK LIFE: "I honor God when I bless others quietly."

....

TALK TO GOD: God, open my eyes to see who I can bless in secret today and how to do that. Amen.

....

REFLECT & RESPOND: How has your generosity been motivated by recognition in the past? How is God calling you to bless another secretly today?

....

DAY 278

Step Out
in Faith

"'Come,' he said. Then Peter got down out of the boat, walked on the water and came toward Jesus. But when he saw the wind, he was afraid and, beginning to sink, cried out, 'Lord, save me!' Immediately Jesus reached out his hand and caught him. 'You of little faith,' he said, 'why did you doubt?'"

Matthew 14:29-31 NIV

Does it feel risky to step out in faith today?

Peter understood. When Jesus invited him to walk on the water, he had a choice: stay safe in the boat or step into the unknown. With his eyes fixed on Jesus, Peter experienced the miraculous—his feet on top of the waves. However, when his focus shifted to the storm, fear filled him, and he began to sink.

Here's the beautiful truth: Jesus didn't let him drown. He honored Peter's faith by reaching out and rescuing him. Peter faltered, but he was still the only one who experienced walking on the water with Jesus in that moment.

God meets us in the unknown with His presence and power. Don't be afraid to step out today.

SPEAK LIFE: "I trust Jesus to meet me in the unknown."

TALK TO GOD: God, guide me to keep my eyes fixed on You. I trust You will meet me as I step into the unknown. Amen.

REFLECT & RESPOND: Where is God calling you to step out in faith? How can you respond, even if it feels risky?

DAY 279

Reflect

Take a few moments to revisit the days you've just walked. There's no rush here—just honesty and grace. Feel free to journal your answers.

Reflection Prompts:

- ✓ What truth stood out to me this week?
- ✓ Where did I notice God inviting me to stop settling?
- ✓ What challenged me? What encouraged me?
- ✓ What thought/encouragement/hope do I want to carry with me into the coming days?

DAY 280

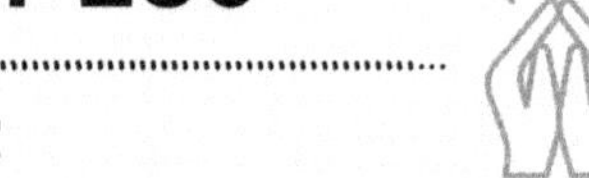

Rest

Today is a day to rest—not to catch up, fix something, or prove anything. Abundant life includes stopping long enough to receive what God is already offering you.

Sit quietly with God for a few minutes.

Breathe deeply.

Allow any Scripture from the past few days to encourage you.

Let yourself be loved and cared for by your Creator.

DAY 281

Refrain from Speaking Defeat

"But we continue to preach because we have the same kind of faith the psalmist had when he said, I believed in God, so I spoke.'"

2 Corinthians 4:13 NLT

Has defeat slipped into your vocabulary?

Since you belong to Jesus, defeat doesn't fit in your language. The enemy of your soul wants you to dwell on and speak words of despair, discouragement, and overwhelm. God, on the other hand, has blessed you with a spirit of faith, not defeat. He has filled you with words of life—words that reflect your belief in Him.

Speaking defeat grows hopelessness, but speaking faith activates the opposite. It activates courage, hope, and perseverance. The truth is, your words don't just describe your reality; they shape it.

When you feel tempted to say something like, "I can't do this," or "My situation will never change," stop and pause. Then ask yourself, "Is this what God says?" Faith speaks God's truth, even when circumstances appear hopeless. Choose to speak victory, strength, and hope today. Defeat is not yours, so refrain from speaking it.

SPEAK LIFE: "My words of faith reflect my belief in Jesus."

TALK TO GOD: Lord, when I begin to say words of defeat, remind me they have no place in my life. Amen.

REFLECT & RESPOND: What is one truth from God's Word that you can speak today? Say it out loud whenever defeat tries to take residence.

DAY 282

Run Your Race with Purpose

"Therefore, since we are surrounded by such a huge crowd of witnesses to the life of faith, let us strip off every weight that slows us down, especially the sin that so easily trips us up. And let us run with endurance the race God has set before us."

Hebrews 12:1 NLT

Ever feel like you're running this race of life alone?

Good news! You're not. Hebrews 12 is a reminder to run with endurance and keep your eyes fixed on the finish line. The "cloud of witnesses," those who have gone before you, surround and encourage you. Their lives prove that a heart surrendered to God bears fruit, perseverance, and a legacy that outlasts time.

Every step of faith matters. Even the quiet ones of prayer, obedience, and love build a life that honors Him. When the road feels long or heavy, remember you're part of a greater story of faith.

Keep running with purpose and hope. Each faithful step draws you closer to the joy set before you, and your race will inspire others to keep going, too.

SPEAK LIFE: "I persevere in my race, focused on Jesus."

TALK TO GOD: Lord, strengthen me as the cloud of witnesses motivates me to keep going. Help me finish my race well. Amen.

REFLECT & RESPOND: What step can you take today with intentional faith? How can you encourage someone else in their race this week?

DAY 283

Overflow with Hope

"May the God of hope fill you with all joy and peace as you trust in him, so that you may overflow with hope by the power of the Holy Spirit."

Romans 15:13 NIV

How hopeful are you today?

We may think of hope as wishing for the best or desiring for things to turn out the way we want. True hope, found in Jesus, is much more. It's solid, secure, and active. God Himself, is the source of this hope, filling us with joy and peace so that it overflows to others.

Notice the connection: as you trust Him, His Spirit works within you, replacing chaos with peace, sorrow with joy, and despair with hope. This isn't something you muster up. It's something He develops in you.

Even when circumstances feel hopeless, hope is not lost. You are never without it because you are never without Him. The God of hope is active in your story, always present and at work.

Take courage today. Let Him fill your heart again. Hope isn't running out; it's running over.

SPEAK LIFE: "God is the source of my never-ending hope."

TALK TO GOD: Lord, when I feel hopeless and helpless, remind me that because I always have You, I always have hope. Amen.

REFLECT & RESPOND: Where are you lacking hope in your life? Take a moment to pray Romans 15:13 over yourself, asking God to fill you.

DAY 284

Recognize Lies to Live Free

"... Then you will know the truth, and the truth will set you free."

John 8:32 NIV

What lies have you been believing lately?

Some settle in so discreetly we don't even recognize them. *You're not talented enough. You'll never change. You're not worthy of love. If they only knew what you did.* These lies, once planted in our minds, can shape the way we see ourselves, others, and God—without us even realizing it.

Jesus doesn't entertain lies. He, instead, breaks them with truth. He tells us that we can, too.

Truth isn't just correct information. Truth is a Person—Jesus. The more time we spend with Him, the clearer His truth becomes in our lives. He reveals the lies we've believed, then He gently replaces them with His truth.

Living free starts with recognizing the lies that have held you captive. Think for a moment. What have you accepted as true that God never said about you?

God created you to live in His truth and to live free. Allow His words to be the ones you believe today.

SPEAK LIFE: "I refuse to live by lies, but instead, walk in truth."

TALK TO GOD: Lord God, fill my mind with Your truth to replace the lies that attempt to tear me down. Amen.

REFLECT & RESPOND: What lies are you believing today? What truth of God speaks louder?

DAY 285

Connect with Your Source

"Remain in me, as I also remain in you. No branch can bear fruit by itself; it must remain in the vine. Neither can you bear fruit unless you remain in me."

John 15:4 NIV

When have you been tempted to go it alone?

God designed you for connection—with Him, with others, with purpose. In a world that entices you to separate, His warm invitation beckons, *Stay with Me.*

Jesus uses the image of the vine and branches to show your connection to Him is vital. A branch doesn't grow on its own; it stays attached to its source. Similarly, your strength, your nourishment, your peace and purpose are found in your Source. Not in hustling harder, not in doing more, but rather in staying connected to Jesus.

Some days when you're overwhelmed, ashamed, or distracted, it feels easier to detach. Yet, that's when you need your Vine, your Lifeline, the most. These times are when your Source steadies you, grows you, and bears fruit through you.

Today, connect with the One your soul clings to—by design. Then watch Him produce in your life what only He can do.

SPEAK LIFE: "I grow by staying connected to Jesus."

TALK TO GOD: Jesus, keep me close, and show me how to daily remain connected with You. Amen.

REFLECT & RESPOND: What helps you feel most connected to Jesus? What might be getting in the way right now?

DAY 286

Reflect

Take a few moments to revisit the days you've just walked. There's no rush here—just honesty and grace. Feel free to journal your answers.

Reflection Prompts:

- ✓ What truth stood out to me this week?
- ✓ Where did I notice God inviting me to stop settling?
- ✓ What challenged me? What encouraged me?
- ✓ What thought/encouragement/hope do I want to carry with me into the coming days?

DAY 287

Rest

Today is a day to rest—not to catch up, fix something, or prove anything. Abundant life includes stopping long enough to receive what God is already offering you.

Sit quietly with God for a few minutes.

Breathe deeply.

Allow any Scripture from the past few days to encourage you.

Let yourself be loved and cared for by your Creator.

DAY 288

Choose to Be Teachable

"Show me your ways, Lord, teach me your paths. Guide me in your truth and teach me, for you are God my Savior, and my hope is in you all day long."

Psalm 25:4-5 NIV

With God, are you more focused on getting results or learning from Him?

David's prayer isn't hurried or demanding. It's humble. He doesn't ask for shortcuts or explanations; he asks to be taught. This teaches us an important truth. God's guidance is less about information and more about relationship.

To ask God to teach you is to admit you don't have it all figured out. This may seem like weakness, but it's actually wisdom. God delights in leading those who are willing to learn, not those who try to be in control. His truth doesn't just direct you, but it shapes who you become along the way.

Notice where David places his hope—not in the results, the timing, or the understanding, but rather in God Himself. *All day long.*

Today, choose to be teachable. Allow God to transform your heart as He guides your steps. He will fill your life with hope.

SPEAK LIFE: "God teaches me and guides me in every step."

TALK TO GOD: Lord, when I seek Your guidance, continue to grow me and my relationship with You. Amen.

REFLECT & RESPOND: What are you seeking God for right now? How will you allow Him to teach you through your current circumstances?

DAY 289

Experience Perfect Peace

"You will keep in perfect peace all who trust in you, all whose thoughts are fixed on you!"

Isaiah 26:3 NLT

How long has it been since you experienced lasting peace?

Isaiah reminds us from where true peace comes. It's found in trusting God and fixing our thoughts on Him. That's it. He does the rest; He keeps us in perfect peace. This is a promise, and it's not for a select few. It's for all.

Trust takes the confidence we have in our own strength and shifts it to Him. Fixing our thoughts on Him means choosing where our mind will rest. We rest on His promises rather than our problems, on His character instead of our concerns. This combination opens the door for God's peace to remain with us, and the good news is, He'll keep us in His perfect peace.

Today, shift your focus back to Him. Choose trust when worries encroach. Cling to His truth when distractions entice your thoughts. As you do, you'll experience the kind of peace only He can give—perfect, lasting, and sure.

SPEAK LIFE: "As I trust God and fix my thoughts on Him, He keeps me in perfect peace."

TALK TO GOD: Lord, remind me to keep trusting You and fixing my thoughts only on You today. Amen.

REFLECT & RESPOND: What keeps you from trusting God? How can you keep your mind centered on Him and His truth?

DAY 290

Grumble Less, Praise More

"In the desert the whole community grumbled against Moses and Aaron. The Israelites said to them, 'If only we had died by the Lord's hand in Egypt! There we sat around pots of meat and ate all the food we wanted, but you have brought us out into this desert to starve this entire assembly to death.'"

Exodus 16:2-3 NIV

Does grumbling escape easily from you?

A few short weeks after crossing the Red Sea, the Israelites complained about food. If we're honest, we might have joined them—already hungry and wishing for what had been. Complaining comes easy, but it never brings us joy, does it? It keeps our focus on what's missing instead of what God provides.

In the verse following this, God's response was one filled with grace and purpose, daily giving them bread from heaven while using it to build their trust. Gratitude does the same for us. Each time we swap grumbling for thanks, we see His faithfulness more clearly, and His joy within us grows.

Today is a good day to grumble less and praise more. Try a little "grumble fast." Exchange every complaint for praise, then watch how it shifts your perspective.

SPEAK LIFE: "Today I choose gratitude over grumbling."

TALK TO GOD: God, remind me that gratefulness honors You and gives me joy. Amen.

REFLECT & RESPOND: Where do you tend to grumble the most? How could you turn it into praise instead?

DAY 291

Walk in His Good Way

"This is what the Lord says: 'Stand at the crossroads and look; ask for the ancient paths, ask where the good way is, and walk in it, and you will find rest for your souls …'"

Jeremiah 6:16a NIV

When was the last time you paused to find your purpose?

Our culture celebrates activity as the basis for importance and success. Yet, God's Word reminds us that constant motion doesn't equal abundant living. Life that is continually on the go—even with good and godly activities—can still feel empty and far from the life God has designed.

Jeremiah offers this invitation: pause, look, and ask. Hectic living can keep us from noticing the crossroads in our lives, but God calls us to pause and seek Him and His direction. Unlike the world, He doesn't reward frantic striving. He promises rest for our souls when we walk in His good way.

Your purpose isn't found in your packed schedule, but instead in walking humbly with God. Trade endless activity for His peaceful presence. Your steps will become more purposeful, intentional, and hopeful.

SPEAK LIFE: "My purpose comes from God, not my schedule."

TALK TO GOD: Lord, guide me to pause today and seek Your will in every area of my life. I want to honor You. Amen.

REFLECT & RESPOND: Where have you confused hectic living with purpose? What would it look like to pause today and seek God's good way?

DAY 292

Let Just Enough Be Enough

"O God, I beg two favors from you; let me have them before I die. First, help me never to tell a lie. Second, give me neither poverty nor riches! Give me just enough to satisfy my needs. For if I grow rich, I may deny you and say, 'Who is the Lord?' And if I am too poor, I may steal and thus insult God's holy name."

Proverbs 30:7-9 NLT

What does "just enough" look like in your life right now?

We don't just stumble upon contentment or discover it one day. We learn contentment slowly along the way.

Agur's prayer in Proverbs reminds us of this truth. He asks for "just enough." His heart isn't restless, chasing more. It's trained to trust God's will and daily provision.

Contentment grows as we learn to let go of what we think we need and simply receive God's best. It's formed in the quiet moments of choosing trust over producing, and gratitude over grumbling.

Learning contentment requires patience—with God, with our circumstances, and with ourselves. Our "just enough" always leads to abundance.

SPEAK LIFE: "God's provision and His best for me is enough."

TALK TO GOD: Lord, continue to teach me how to be content and to trust Your provision. Amen.

REFLECT & RESPOND: Where is God inviting you to practice contentment right now? How will you trust His provision?

DAY 293

Reflect

Take a few moments to revisit the days you've just walked. There's no rush here—just honesty and grace. Feel free to journal your answers.

Reflection Prompts:

- ✓ What truth stood out to me this week?
- ✓ Where did I notice God inviting me to stop settling?
- ✓ What challenged me? What encouraged me?
- ✓ What thought/encouragement/hope do I want to carry with me into the coming days?

DAY 294

Rest

Today is a day to rest—not to catch up, fix something, or prove anything. Abundant life includes stopping long enough to receive what God is already offering you.

Sit quietly with God for a few minutes.

Breathe deeply.

Allow any Scripture from the past few days to encourage you.

Let yourself be loved and cared for by your Creator.

DAY 295

Fill Your Mouth with Praise

*"I will praise the Lord at all times.
I will constantly speak his praises."*

Psalm 34:1 NLT

Do you speak most often in criticism or praise?

David declared he would continually praise the Lord, not just when life was easy or pleasant—but at all times. He knew this truth: praise isn't dependent on our circumstances, but it's a choice that switches our perspective from our problems to our Provider.

Isn't it interesting that when we speak praises, we become more joyful? Praise eliminates fear, invites God's presence, and keeps our focus on His goodness. Criticism drains us, but praise strengthens us. Worry conflicts us, but worship frees us.

Even when life is difficult, we can choose to speak words of worship. "Lord, You are faithful. Lord, You are good. Lord, You are worthy." These declarations keep truth and hope at the front and center.

Today, instead of allowing negativity or discouragement to mold your words, choose to fill your mouth with praise. In doing so, you live full of joy with a renewed faith.

SPEAK LIFE: "My mouth is full of praise today."

TALK TO GOD: Lord, fill my mouth with praise throughout this day. May it become a beautiful habit in my everyday life. Amen.

REFLECT & RESPOND: What words have filled your mouth most recently? Take a moment now to speak a word of praise out loud.

DAY 296

Offer Encouragement Generously

"Let us think of ways to motivate one another to acts of love and good works. And let us not neglect our meeting together, as some people do, but encourage one another, especially now that the day of his return is drawing near."

Hebrews 10:24-25 NLT

What if your encouraging words made the difference for another today?

Encouragement is a beautiful gift; yet, it can transform a heart, change a perspective, or strengthen a weary soul. More than words that make us feel good, encouragement is biblical. Scripture reminds us to intentionally connect, motivate plentifully, and encourage one another in godly ways.

Offering encouragement may be noticing the unique ways God is working in someone's life and speaking truth over her. It may be a text, note, smile, or simply reminding others you see them, and they matter. Other times, it's helping, listening, or praying for someone openly.

When you encourage generously, you create a ripple effect. Your words can inspire courage, build belief, and point someone to Jesus. Never underestimate the power of encouragement from your soul to another.

SPEAK LIFE: "Today I will encourage others generously."

TALK TO GOD: Lord, guide me to whoever needs encouragement today. Give me the words they need to hear. Amen.

REFLECT & RESPOND: Who in your life needs encouragement today? How is God calling you to be the one to encourage?

DAY 297

Trust When You're Afraid

"When I am afraid, I put my trust in you. In God, whose word I praise—in God I trust and am not afraid. What can mere mortals do to me?"

Psalm 56:3-4 NIV

What are you fearing today?

Fear clouds your view, whispering doubts about your abilities, your future, and even God's promises. The Psalmist here offers this powerful and practical strategy: when you're afraid, trust in God. Each time you choose to rely on God, you weaken fear's presence.

Faith doesn't ignore danger or difficulties, but it sees them through to God's power and presence. Fear wants to paralyze you; faith prompts you to move forward.

Notice how the second part of the verse refers to praising God. Interestingly, praise and trust are inseparable. Speaking truth in praise over your circumstances shifts your perspective from worry to hope. Fear dissipates when faith is firm. With God, fear has no power over you.

SPEAK LIFE: "I choose to trust God, and in Him I have nothing to fear."

TALK TO GOD: Lord God, when fear tries to paralyze me, fill me with confident faith in You. I have nothing to fear with You. Amen.

REFLECT & RESPOND: What fear is trying to control your thoughts right now? How can you actively replace it with faith and trust in God today?

DAY 298

Invest in the Eternal

"The world and its desires pass away, but whoever does the will of God lives forever."

1 John 2:17 NIV

How are you aligning yourself with God's plans today?

Everything in this world has an expiration date. Careers, possessions, accolades, and even relationships can fade or change. The challenge is not to just remove these expiring things, but instead to decide where to place your energy, attention, and devotion. John points out that those who align with God are connected to what never fades—the eternal.

Investing in the eternal doesn't require elaborate giving. It can result from consistent faithfulness, daily obedience, and small acts of love that point to God. Each choice—how we spend our time, how we speak, what we prioritize—is an opportunity to put our energy into what truly matters.

Ask yourself this question: *Am I pouring my heart into things that pass away, or am I intentionally aligning with God's plans and purposes?* When you invest wisely, God turns ordinary into extraordinary, and your life makes an impact in His kingdom. No expiring thing can touch that.

SPEAK LIFE: "Today I invest in what lasts."

TALK TO GOD: God, help me to do Your will and to focus on what's eternal, not in what expires. Amen.

REFLECT & RESPOND: How can you redirect yourself toward eternal priorities today? Which small, intentional action can you take now to invest in what lasts?

DAY 299

Watch God's Word at Work

"It is the same with my word. I send it out, and it always produces fruit. It will accomplish all I want it to, and it will prosper everywhere I send it."

Isaiah 55:11 NLT

Do you ever wonder if God's Word is really working in your life?

Sometimes we read Scripture, pray it, and even speak it aloud, yet we don't immediately see results. We may wonder if anything is happening. Isaiah reminds us that God's Word always accomplishes its purpose. His promises don't expire, His truth doesn't fade, and His voice never fails to bring life.

Even when you don't see it, God is working. Every verse planted in your heart grows in His timing. Every truth spoken in faith contains His power. His Word restores, strengthens, convicts, comforts, and brings fruit in His perfect timing.

Continue reading, believing, and speaking His Word. Trust that what He has spoken over you is already bearing fruit. His Word never misses its target, and neither will His purpose for you.

SPEAK LIFE: "God's Word is at work in my life."

TALK TO GOD: Lord, thank You for Your Word, and for the reminder that You work through it, even when I don't see it. Amen.

REFLECT & RESPOND: Where do you need to stand firm on God's Word today? Write down a promise from Scripture you can cling to this week.

DAY 300

Reflect

Take a few moments to revisit the days you've just walked. There's no rush here—just honesty and grace. Feel free to journal your answers.

Reflection Prompts:

- ✓ What truth stood out to me this week?
- ✓ Where did I notice God inviting me to stop settling?
- ✓ What challenged me? What encouraged me?
- ✓ What thought/encouragement/hope do I want to carry with me into the coming days?

DAY 301

Rest

Today is a day to rest—not to catch up, fix something, or prove anything. Abundant life includes stopping long enough to receive what God is already offering you.

Sit quietly with God for a few minutes.

Breathe deeply.

Allow any Scripture from the past few days to encourage you.

Let yourself be loved and cared for by your Creator.

DAY 302

Hear Him Singing Over You

"'… The Lord your God is with you, the Mighty Warrior who saves. He will take great delight in you; in his love he will no longer rebuke you, but will rejoice over you with singing.'"

Zephaniah 3:17 NIV

Do you ever imagine God smiling when He thinks of you?

We may believe the truth that God loves us, yet also believe He's disappointed or frustrated with us. Zephaniah gives us a different picture. He creates the image, not of a rigid father, but rather of a Mighty Warrior Who fights for us and a Heavenly Father Who sings over us with joy.

Get this: He doesn't simply forgive you; He delights in you. He doesn't simply accept you; He celebrates you. His song over you isn't based on what you do or don't do. It comes naturally from His heart because He loves you fully.

Allow this to sink in, and hear Him singing over you. You are loved, delighted in, and held securely in His hands. Walk into today not as someone God merely tolerates, but as someone over whom He rejoices.

SPEAK LIFE: "God smiles when He thinks of me."

TALK TO GOD: Lord, when I begin to think You're frustrated with me, prompt me to remember You take great delight in me. Amen.

REFLECT & RESPOND: How have you been believing God is disappointed in you lately? Pray a short prayer based on Zephaniah 3:17.

DAY 303

Return,
Rest,
Remain

"'I am the vine; you are the branches. If you remain in me and I in you, you will bear much fruit; apart from me you can do nothing...'"

John 15:5 NIV

Have you noticed how easy it is to drift from God without meaning to?

He knows our tendencies and how quickly we get distracted. He knows that, apart from Him, life feels hollow and difficult. His desire is always to draw us back.

We can't create peace, joy, or purpose on our own. Nor can we thrive the way we're designed. That's why Jesus reminds us of this truth: apart from Him, we can do nothing.

To remain in Him means to stay, to dwell, to make your home. It's simply being with Him—drawing life and strength from your Vine.

The secret is this: when you stay connected, fruit appears. Peace returns. Hope abounds. Just as a branch can't live without the vine, we can't thrive without Jesus.

Even if you've wandered, He won't cut you off from Him. His invitation to return, rest, and remain is always open to you. With Him, your soul finds abundant life.

SPEAK LIFE: "I choose to remain in Jesus today."

TALK TO GOD: Jesus, when I wander, guide me to return, rest, and remain in You. Amen.

REFLECT & RESPOND: Have you drifted from Jesus lately? What's one step you can take to return and remain in Him?

DAY 304

Trust and Live Free

"Trust in the Lord with all your heart and lean not on your own understanding; in all your ways submit to him, and he will make your paths straight."

Proverbs 3:5-6 NIV

Trusting God isn't always easy, is it?

It may feel risky at times, even foolish. However, it leads us to true freedom. When we rely on our own understanding, we carry the pressure of figuring everything out by ourselves. The wisdom of Proverbs reminds us that when we trust God fully, He leads us in ways no one else can—not even ourselves.

Trusting the Lord doesn't mean He'll reveal the full plan in advance, but it does mean you believe the One leading you knows the way. As you release control and let Him guide your steps, you'll experience unexpected peace. With that peace comes freedom—freedom from worry, striving, and the need to hold everything together on your own.

You don't have to know how it will all work out. You only need to remember Who you're walking beside. Enjoy the freedom of trust today.

SPEAK LIFE: "As I trust God, He leads me into true freedom."

TALK TO GOD: Lord, lead my heart to trust You fully in all things today. Amen.

REFLECT & RESPOND: Where do you struggle with trusting God? Pause and ask Him to help you trust Him fully today.

DAY 305

Number Your Days

"Teach us to number our days, that we may gain a heart of wisdom."

Psalm 90:12 NIV

When was the last time you pondered the brevity of your life?

Moses reminds us that when we recognize how short our time is on this earth, we seek God's wisdom to live out our days well. Not in our own ways and with our own desires, but rather in alignment with God's. Instead of cramming in more, we ask God to help us live out His will.

This reality isn't meant to be depressing; it's meant to be motivating and encouraging. It prompts us to live intentionally every single day, to invest in what matters most—relationships, serving, rest, and growing closer to God—all while seeking God for His wisdom.

No, we don't control the length of our days, but we get to choose what we do in them. Numbering our days enables us to put God, His will, and His ways at the center of all we do. This can't help but make an eternal impact today.

SPEAK LIFE: "I seek God's wisdom to live out the length of my days."

TALK TO GOD: God, give me a heart of wisdom to live out this day well with You. Help me to glorify You. Amen.

REFLECT & RESPOND: What's one way you could align your day with God's will? How will you intentionally seek His wisdom?

DAY 306

Choose Rhythm Over Routines

"God called the light 'day,' and the darkness 'night.' And evening passed and morning came, marking the first day... Then God looked over all he had made, and he saw that it was very good!"

Genesis 1:5, 31a NLT

Does your life ever feel like it's an endless checklist of tasks?

From the very beginning, God created everything with rhythms—light and dark, work and rest, evening and morning. His perfect design shows His order and His intentional flow in the rhythms of life.

Too often, however, we slip into survival-mode routines. We measure our days by productivity instead of staying present. Yet, God's creation account shows us a different way. Each rhythm has a purpose, and each cycle has an order; when we align ourselves with them, we find a healthier, more sustainable way of living.

Choosing rhythm over routine is about aligning our lives to God's design, not forcing ourselves into patterns that drain us. Listening, responding, and moving in sync with our Creator enables us to live the life He calls "very good."

SPEAK LIFE: "God designed me for healthy rhythms, not relentless routines."

TALK TO GOD: God, I can get stuck in routines that run me weary. Teach me Your rhythms and guide me to live in them. Amen.

REFLECT & RESPOND: Where are you clinging to rigid routines that leave you weary? How can you invite God's rhythms into your days?

DAY 307

Reflect

Take a few moments to revisit the days you've just walked. There's no rush here—just honesty and grace. Feel free to journal your answers.

Reflection Prompts:

- ✓ What truth stood out to me this week?
- ✓ Where did I notice God inviting me to stop settling?
- ✓ What challenged me? What encouraged me?
- ✓ What thought/encouragement/hope do I want to carry with me into the coming days?

DAY 308

Rest

Today is a day to rest—not to catch up, fix something, or prove anything. Abundant life includes stopping long enough to receive what God is already offering you.

Sit quietly with God for a few minutes.

Breathe deeply.

Allow any Scripture from the past few days to encourage you.

Let yourself be loved and cared for by your Creator.

DAY 309

Make Yourself Available

"Then I heard the voice of the Lord saying, 'Whom shall I send? And who will go for us?' And I said, 'Here am I. Send me!'"

Isaiah 6:8 NIV

When was the last time you offered to God, "Here am I"?

Have you ever? Isaiah's response wasn't polished. It simply came from a willing heart—and that was enough.

God's call often seems bigger than our capabilities. It can cause us to feel vulnerable and uncomfortable. Yet, Scripture reminds us that God equips those He calls. When we make ourselves available, He provides all we need and even what we lack.

Making yourself available to God doesn't mean you feel ready or that you know what to expect. It does mean, however, that you trust God's strength will meet you in your present circumstance. This simple act can set His purposes in motion through your life in ways you could never predict.

Today, listen for His call. When you hear it, dare to answer with the same bold words: "Here am I. Send me."

SPEAK LIFE: "I make myself available to God, even when it's uncomfortable."

TALK TO GOD: God, help me to never hesitate when You call me forward. Give me what I need to follow You. Amen.

REFLECT & RESPOND: What is God asking you to do today? How can you step forward in faith even when you feel uncertain?

DAY 310

Don't Miss Today While Chasing Tomorrow

"For he says, 'In the time of my favor I heard you, and in the day of salvation I helped you.' I tell you, now is the time of God's favor, now is the day of salvation."

2 Corinthians 6:2 NIV

Do you ever catch yourself waiting for "someday" to finally feel content?

We might tell ourselves that life will be better once tomorrow comes. Once the kids grow up, once the position is achieved, once the season changes—then we'll feel settled and satisfied. This kind of thinking always keeps joy and peace just out of reach.

Paul tells us we no longer have to wait. God's favor and salvation are not for a future moment; they are already here today. We experience contentment when we stop striving for "someday" and start embracing the goodness God has for us now.

Don't miss today as you chase after tomorrow. Don't live discontented now, waiting for life to line up perfectly. Rest in the truth that God's presence, provision, and promises are perfect and enough for you right now.

SPEAK LIFE: "God's favor is with me, so I choose to be content."

TALK TO GOD: Lord God, remind me I can be content in every situation because of Your peace, provision, and presence right now. Amen.

REFLECT & RESPOND: How have you been waiting for "someday" to finally feel content? What can you do to see today as already enough?

DAY 311

Speak From the Overflow

"A good person produces good things from the treasury of a good heart, and an evil person produces evil things from the treasury of an evil heart. What you say flows from what is in your heart."

Luke 6:45 NLT

What fills your heart?

Jesus makes it clear. What's inside our hearts flows through our mouths. If our hearts are full of bitterness, fear, or worry, our words will be also. Likewise, if our hearts are filled with God's truth, love, and hope, then our words will communicate life.

It's important to guard and care for our hearts. By spending time in God's Word, praying, worshipping, and surrounding ourselves with godly encouragement, this influence overflows into our lives—and out into the lives of others around us.

Consider for a moment what is overflowing from you. If your words have been sharp, negative, or critical, perhaps it's time for a fresh filling of God's Spirit. Invite Him to cleanse, renew, and refill your heart so that your words will offer His life-giving truth.

SPEAK LIFE: "I fill my heart with God's love and Word."

TALK TO GOD: Lord, show me what is in my heart. Fill me to overflowing with Your love and compassion. Amen.

REFLECT & RESPOND: What are your words revealing about what's in your heart? How can you invite God to fill you so that your overflow blesses others?

DAY 312

Put Others First

"Don't be selfish; don't try to impress others. Be humble, thinking of others as better than yourselves. Don't look out only for your own interests, but take an interest in others, too."

Philippians 2:3-4 NLT

When was the last time you intentionally put someone else ahead of yourself?

In a world that emphasizes being first, serving for recognition, and doing only what benefits ourselves, humility is looked upon as weakness. Paul, however, points us to a counter-cultural way to live—to put others ahead of ourselves.

Humility doesn't come easy, though, does it? It's a choice we make daily. We choose to give credit to another, to bless without expectation, to listen fully engaged, and to celebrate someone's success without comparison.

Jesus modeled this perfectly. Though He was God, He came to serve and love without strings attached. He always put others ahead of Himself. Each time we do this, too, we emulate Him.

Today, look for opportunities to put others first, and watch what God does through you.

SPEAK LIFE: "Today I will put others ahead of myself."

TALK TO GOD: Lord, help me to live the way Jesus lived: humble, open, and focused on others. Amen.

REFLECT & RESPOND: Where in your life do you tend to put yourself above others? What's one thing you can do today to put someone else first?

DAY 313

Listen for His Voice

"My sheep listen to my voice; I know them, and they follow me."

John 10:27 NIV

What voice are you hearing today?

In the midst of today's noise—emails, social media, people's opinions—God's voice can sound quiet. Yet, Jesus declares that His sheep listen to His Voice, He knows them, and they follow Him.

Hearing His voice requires stillness. It means pausing long enough to distinguish His voice from the world's clamour. The rewards of hearing from Him are confidence, courage, and creativity—none of which come from your striving, your schedule, or your own strength. These gifts come from responding to His guidance. You experience a vibrant intimacy with Him. His voice guides, corrects, and comforts. The more you follow, the more you recognize Him, His heart, and His wisdom.

Faith grows in the act of following. God knows you personally, and He invites you into His abundance. Trust that His guidance is perfect and worth every pause, every step, and every act of obedience.

Listen for His voice today.

SPEAK LIFE: "When the world is loud, I pause to listen for God's voice."

TALK TO GOD: Lord, prompt me to pause throughout this day to hear Your voice. Help me follow where you lead. Amen.

REFLECT & RESPOND: How can you tangibly pause today to hear God more clearly? What is one way you can follow His direction right now?

DAY 314

Reflect

Take a few moments to revisit the days you've just walked. There's no rush here—just honesty and grace. Feel free to journal your answers.

Reflection Prompts:

- ✓ What truth stood out to me this week?
- ✓ Where did I notice God inviting me to stop settling?
- ✓ What challenged me? What encouraged me?
- ✓ What thought/encouragement/hope do I want to carry with me into the coming days?

DAY 315

Rest

Today is a day to rest—not to catch up, fix something, or prove anything. Abundant life includes stopping long enough to receive what God is already offering you.

Sit quietly with God for a few minutes.

Breathe deeply.

Allow any Scripture from the past few days to encourage you.

Let yourself be loved and cared for by your Creator.

DAY 316

Center Your Life on the Lamb

"After this I saw a vast crowd, too great to count, from every nation and tribe and people and language, standing in front of the throne and before the Lamb. They were clothed in white robes and held palm branches in their hands. And they were shouting with a great roar, 'Salvation comes from our God who sits on the throne and from the Lamb!'"

Revelation 7:9-10 NLT

Does life feel heavy today?

John's vision in Revelation gives us a breathtaking glimpse of eternity. We see a countless multitude, united in worship, voices lifted as one. *Can you imagine?*

Not us, our accomplishments, our perseverance—none are at the center of this heavenly scene. None but the Lamb, Jesus. The One Who was slain, Who purchased our freedom, and Who conquered death, stands alone as the focus of eternal adoration. Every voice and every heart bow before Him.

When life feels noisy or heavy, remember everything is centered on the Lamb on the throne. If eternity centers on Jesus, so can today. Allow your heart to reflect that worship. Lift your voice. Fix your eyes. Live in awe.

SPEAK LIFE: "My heart is centered on Jesus today."

TALK TO GOD: Lord, thank You for this glimpse of my future. Remind me of it when life gets heavy. Amen.

REFLECT & RESPOND: How does this vision of eternity encourage you? What can you do now to center your heart on Jesus?

DAY 317

Live in What God Has Given You

"For God has not given us a spirit of fear and timidity, but of power, love, and self-discipline."

2 Timothy 1:7 NLT

Has fear been knocking on the door of your heart?

Fear has a way of creeping in and telling us that we don't have what it takes, that we might not make it, or that it's safer not to step out in faith. Paul reminds Timothy—and us—that fear is not from God. If it doesn't come from Him, we don't have to receive it.

God, instead, has given us a spirit of power, love, and self-discipline. Power to face challenges with courage. Love that casts out fear and extends grace to others. Self-discipline to walk in wisdom and live with focus, not in chaos.

Even in moments of trembling, you don't have to let fear win. God's Spirit within you is greater. You are empowered, equipped, and dearly loved.

Walk boldly in this truth today: God has already given you everything you need to live with courage and hope. Abundant life is yours.

SPEAK LIFE: "I walk in power, love, and self-discipline today."

TALK TO GOD: God, as I journey through this day, guide me in Your power, love, and self-discipline, no matter what I face. Amen.

REFLECT & RESPOND: Where are you letting fear run and rule your life? How can you rely on God's Spirit of power and love instead?

DAY 318

Unpack What You've Been Carrying

"Cast your cares on the Lord and he will sustain you; he will never let the righteous be shaken."

Psalm 55:22 NIV

How would you feel if you let go of all you've been carrying?

You've been carrying more than anyone realizes—even yourself. Expectations. Guilt. Pressure to keep it all together. Old wounds you've stuffed down. Fears that whisper at night. Responsibilities that weigh more than you admit—or even recognize.

God sees it all.

Not with judgment, but He looks through eyes of love. He invites you to unload it all into His capable hands—to cast them, to hurl them onto Him. Why? Because He will sustain you. He will help you. You weren't designed to carry such a load, but you were created to be carried by the One Who can.

Allow today to be a turning point. You don't need to stay strong or pretend any longer. You are safe to bring it all and give it to Him. Every single part. Every single care. Unpack it all with Him. He's ready to receive it.

SPEAK LIFE: "I cast my cares on the One Who cares for me."

TALK TO GOD: God, I give my cares to you. Please bring healing where needed, hope to my soul, and rest for my weariness. Amen.

REFLECT & RESPOND: Take a few quiet minutes to name what you've been carrying. Then release it all in prayer—imperfectly, honestly, freely.

DAY 319

Say Yes and Follow Him

"Then he said to the crowd, 'If any of you wants to be my follower, you must give up your own way, take up your cross daily, and follow me ...'"

Luke 9:23 NLT

What does your first "yes" look like each morning?

Is your first yes to your to-do list, your phone, your own plans, or to Jesus? Following Him is a choice—not a one-time event, but rather a simple and powerful yes every day. Some days, that yes feels natural; other days, it feels heavy. Yet, Jesus' call remains the same: release your own way, take up your cross, and follow Him.

This daily yes means trusting His way even when it's inconvenient or unclear. It's believing His plans are good and His presence is sure. Each morning, you are given a fresh opportunity to commit your thoughts, actions, and decisions to Him.

Here's the encouragement: every yes shapes your heart, grows your faith, and draws you closer to God. Just be willing; no need to be perfect. Say yes today, and watch how He meets you.

SPEAK LIFE: "My daily yes to God is the best yes."

TALK TO GOD: Jesus, help me to choose Your way and trust You're leading me to Your best. Amen.

REFLECT & RESPOND: How are you saying yes to Jesus, taking up your cross, and following Him? What difference is this making in your life?

DAY 320

Remember His Faithfulness

"But then I recall all you have done, O Lord; I remember your wonderful deeds of long ago."

Psalm 77:11 NLT

Does your heart feel heavy and your faith small?

It's in these moments when the act of remembering stabilizes us. When we pause to recall God's past faithfulness—the prayers He's answered, the ways He's provided, the times He's brought peace in difficult circumstances—we find the hope and encouragement we need for the present moment.

The Psalmist models this beautifully, choosing to recall and rehearse God's goodness. This is faith in action. When we choose to remember what God has done, our focus shifts from what's uncertain to what's true: God has been faithful before, and He will be faithful again. That's His character. That's who He is. We can count on it.

When you remember God's past faithfulness, gratitude can't help but grow. Hope, then, naturally increases. It's a good day to remember once more. Looking back reminds you that you've seen God move, and you'll see Him again.

SPEAK LIFE: "God has been faithful in the past, and I believe He will be faithful again."

TALK TO GOD: God, You are faithful. Remind me when I forget. I trust You will be faithful again. Amen.

REFLECT & RESPOND: How has God been faithful to you in the past? What's one way you can thank Him today?

DAY 321

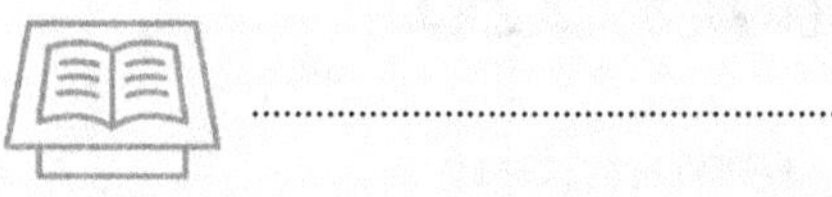

Reflect

Take a few moments to revisit the days you've just walked. There's no rush here—just honesty and grace. Feel free to journal your answers.

Reflection Prompts:

- ✓ What truth stood out to me this week?
- ✓ Where did I notice God inviting me to stop settling?
- ✓ What challenged me? What encouraged me?
- ✓ What thought/encouragement/hope do I want to carry with me into the coming days?

DAY 322

Rest

Today is a day to rest—not to catch up, fix something, or prove anything. Abundant life includes stopping long enough to receive what God is already offering you.

Sit quietly with God for a few minutes.

Breathe deeply.

Allow any Scripture from the past few days to encourage you.

Let yourself be loved and cared for by your Creator.

DAY 323

Live Within God's Design

Isn't it freeing to let go of responsibilities that don't belong to you?

God's boundaries bring this kind of peace. They define what He's entrusted to you—your time, relationships, health, and calling—and protect you from being stretched beyond His plans and purposes. Boundaries aren't barriers to keep you from living; they're guardrails that lead you to abundant life.

When you live inside God's design, you stop carrying responsibilities that aren't yours to bear. You can give your full attention to what He's placed in your hands—growing your faith, loving your people well, and caring for the spaces He's called you to tend. Boundaries also remind you that not everything is yours to fix or manage. This is incredibly freeing.

This is why the Psalmist could call his inheritance "delightful." God's boundaries don't confine; they free you to flourish. Within His design, you'll find clarity, rest, and joy in the life He's given you.

SPEAK LIFE: "God's good design enables me to flourish today."

TALK TO GOD: God, align my priorities with Yours, and help me set boundaries to protect them. Amen.

REFLECT & RESPOND: Where in your life are you needing God's boundaries? How can honoring these boundaries protect what is most important to you and to God?

DAY 324

Realize Your Greatest Gift

"Lord, you alone are my inheritance, my cup of blessing. You guard all that is mine."

Psalm 16:5 NLT

When was the last time you slowed down long enough to recognize that God Himself, is your greatest blessing?

Life can feel complicated some days, and it's often the quiet, simple moments that remind us of His presence. A comforting cup of coffee in the morning, the song of a bird outside the window, or a conversation with a friend who truly listens. These gifts may be bigger than we realize, especially if they appear small in the moment. They point us back to the Giver.

Psalm 16 reminds us that our true inheritance isn't what we accomplish or collect. Rather, it's God Himself. He is our inheritance, our blessing, and the One Who guards all that He's given us.

When we learn to slow down, notice, and treasure both the ordinary and the eternal, our contentment grows. Joy comes not from having more; it comes from realizing we already have the greatest gift of all—God Himself.

SPEAK LIFE: "God is my greatest gift, and in Him I am content."

TALK TO GOD: God, open my eyes to see You as my greatest gift throughout this day. Thank You. Amen.

REFLECT & RESPOND: Take a few moments today to appreciate God's presence in your life. How will you thank Him today?

DAY 325

Be Quick to Listen

"Understand this, my dear brothers and sisters: You must all be quick to listen, slow to speak, and slow to get angry."

James 1:19 NLT

Are you quicker to listen or to speak?

James reminds us the importance of listening in relationships. Listening is not only good for those we're listening to, but it's also good for us. It slows us down. It allows us to receive what others are saying, to understand them better, and to respond graciously.

When we choose to listen first, we stay present better. We show others they matter and that they deserve to be heard. It's another way we honor others with love and appreciation.

Jesus modeled this with His attentiveness to people. He listened first, He noticed details, and then He asked questions. His example encourages us to impact the world around us with ears already engaged.

Today, slow your pace. Be intentional in your conversations. Before planning your reply, listen fully first, and watch what Jesus does through you.

SPEAK LIFE: "Listening first helps me be more like Jesus in my relationships."

TALK TO GOD: God, open my heart to others today, to listen intently first before speaking. Amen.

REFLECT & RESPOND: When has listening first before speaking impacted your relationships for good? How can you practice slowing down to listen today?

DAY 326

Follow God into the Future

"The Lord your God is going ahead of you. He will fight for you, just as you saw him do in Egypt."

Deuteronomy 1:30 NLT

Does the unknown of the future make you nervous?

Deuteronomy 1 declares you don't step into the unknown of tomorrow alone. Think about this: the God Who rescued His people from Egypt and split the sea in two is the same God Who walks ahead of you now.

This means you don't have to live in fear of what's ahead. God not only goes with you, He also goes before you. He fights battles you cannot see, clears paths you didn't know were blocked, and strengthens you every step of the way.

Your future is not uncharted territory to Him. It's already mapped out in His sovereign care. What feels uncertain to you is secure in His hands. That doesn't mean the journey will be easy, but it does mean He's leading you victoriously.

Today, rest in this assurance: God is going before you, and He's leading you to His best.

SPEAK LIFE: "God goes before me today."

TALK TO GOD: Lord, when the future is uncertain, remind me that You are going ahead of me. I trust You. Amen.

REFLECT & RESPOND: With what about the future are you fearful? How can remembering that God goes before you change the way you step into it?

DAY 327

Commit, Trust, and Find Help

"Commit everything you do to the Lord. Trust him, and he will help you."

Psalm 37:5 NLT

Does life feel uncertain, and are worries piling up?

This often happens when we try to do everything on our own. David offers another way in this psalm. Commit everything you do to the Lord. Not just the big things; commit the daily details, too.

Commitment means entrusting your plans, problems, and pace to God, knowing He cares and is capable of handling it all. As you commit, you're also called to trust—that He knows best, even when the outcome isn't clear in the moment.

Trusting God looks like giving Him your fears, disappointments, and unknowns, believing He is already at work on your behalf. His sovereignty is personal, guiding, and kind, and it's one in which you can rest. You no longer have to carry it all.

Here's the promise: when you commit and trust, He helps. Always. Let today be a day of release—a fresh choice to place everything in His hands and rest in His faithful care.

SPEAK LIFE: "I trustfully commit everything to God today."

TALK TO GOD: God, guide me to release everything to You. I trust You will help me. Amen.

REFLECT & RESPOND: What are you having a difficult time committing to God? How will you intentionally choose to trust Him with this?

DAY 328

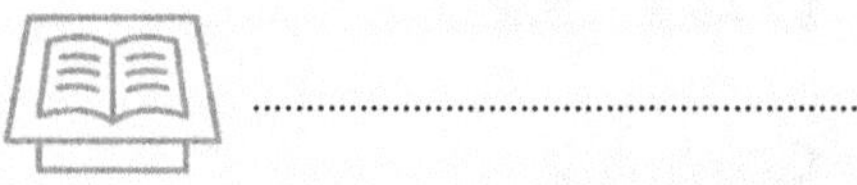

Reflect

Take a few moments to revisit the days you've just walked. There's no rush here—just honesty and grace. Feel free to journal your answers.

Reflection Prompts:

- ✓ What truth stood out to me this week?
- ✓ Where did I notice God inviting me to stop settling?
- ✓ What challenged me? What encouraged me?
- ✓ What thought/encouragement/hope do I want to carry with me into the coming days?

DAY 329

Rest

Today is a day to rest—not to catch up, fix something, or prove anything. Abundant life includes stopping long enough to receive what God is already offering you.

Sit quietly with God for a few minutes.

Breathe deeply.

Allow any Scripture from the past few days to encourage you.

Let yourself be loved and cared for by your Creator.

DAY 330

Run to Him When You Feel Unworthy

"So we praise God for the glorious grace he has poured out on us who belong to his dear Son."

Ephesians 1:6 NLT

When, lately, have you felt unworthy in your everyday life?

The voice of unworthiness isn't always loud; often, it slips in quietly. It may sound like "You haven't prayed enough. You didn't read your Bible today. God cannot use someone like you."

The truth is that God isn't waiting for perfection. He isn't grading your performance or holding out until you get it all together. Instead, He pours out His grace to each who believes in Jesus, because that's Who He is.

You're not barely accepted; you are welcomed by God—wholeheartedly, joyfully, and completely. Grace is God fully seeing you, in all your brokenness and your beauty, choosing you anyway. It's the foundation of your worth and identity, no matter how often unworthiness tries to discourage you or derail you.

The next time you begin to feel unworthy, don't run from God. Run *to* Him. His grace is always waiting for you with open arms.

SPEAK LIFE: "I am worthy because of God and His grace."

TALK TO GOD: Lord God, prompt me to run to You when unworthiness tries to discourage me. Amen.

REFLECT & RESPOND: Write down one lie you've believed about your worth. Talk to God about it, and give that lie to Him.

DAY 331

Draw Near and Stay Close

"Come near to God and he will come near to you."

James 4:8a NIV

Ever wonder if God wants you near?

The world may reject you, ignore you, or push you away, but gratefully, God never does. His desire is to have you close to Him. In fact, James states that when we come near to God, He comes near to us.

God doesn't make it complicated or confusing. He simply calls, *Come.* This invitation isn't a one-time invitation. It's a way of life—staying connected, remembering the location of your true home. Drawing near to God isn't just for crises; it's also for the ordinary mornings, the long afternoons, and the quiet evenings when nothing dramatic is happening.

What happens when you do? He meets you. Every single time. Whether your prayers are bold or barely a whisper, He hears them. Whether your faith feels strong or shaky, He welcomes you.

If you've drifted, now is the perfect time to return. The open arms of your Father welcome you. Draw near and stay close.

SPEAK LIFE: "I'm blessed to remember that God wants me near Him."

TALK TO GOD: Heavenly Father, show me how I can draw near and stay right where I'm designed to be—next to You. Amen.

REFLECT & RESPOND: How is God inviting you closer right now? How will you respond to His invitation?

DAY 332

Allow Him to Be Greater

"He must become greater and greater, and I must become less and less."

John 3:30 NLT

Do you ever desire to be the greatest and most important?

John the Baptist gave us another way. He desired Jesus to become greater and John to become less. This declaration reveals the heart of true spiritual growth—letting go of our own agendas, pride, and control so that God can take center stage in our lives.

Jesus invites us to a life of making space for Him to work fully. When we choose less of ourselves and more of Him, our lives begin to reflect His love, power, and purpose.

This act of humility is not about losing who you are, but instead about finding your true self in Jesus. It's a daily invitation to die to self and rise in Him, allowing His light to shine through you.

As you live this way, you'll find a freedom you've not experienced before, and a deeper, richer relationship with God. Allow Him to be greater.

SPEAK LIFE: "Jesus is first in my life, not me."

TALK TO GOD: Lord, create the desire within me for You to be greater and for me to be less in my life. Amen.

REFLECT & RESPOND: How can you foster a "less of me, more of Him" attitude today? What is standing in the way?

DAY 333

Don't Conform; Be Transformed

"Don't copy the behavior and customs of this world, but let God transform you into a new person by changing the way you think. Then you will learn to know God's will for you, which is good and pleasing and perfect."

Romans 12:2 NLT

What's shaping you more these days—the culture around you or the God within you?

Everything we allow into our lives shapes us—what we listen to, watch, and read. They all impact our thoughts and form our beliefs. Maybe this is why Paul warns against copying the ways of the world. Its distractions and practices can sneakily snatch our focus from God and onto lesser things.

God offers transformation. When you let Him fill your mind with His truth, His promises, and His perspective, He transforms you into someone new. Not just an updated version of yourself, but He makes a brand new one—one that lives differently from the world.

Each day you face a choice: blend in with the world or allow God to change you. Choose the latter, and watch what God does as He leads you to a life that reflects His good, pleasing, and perfect will.

SPEAK LIFE: "I allow God to shape me, not the world."

TALK TO GOD: God, transform me today by changing my thoughts. Amen.

REFLECT & RESPOND: What's been shaping you lately? How can you intentionally turn your focus toward God today?

DAY 334

Write It Down

"After the victory, the Lord instructed Moses, 'Write this down on a scroll as a permanent reminder, and read it aloud to Joshua: I will erase the memory of Amalek from under heaven.'"

Exodus 17:14 NLT

Do you ever struggle with remembering what's important?

We can be forgetful. Not because we don't care; it's because life is loud and distracting. God knows this about us, which may be why He often told His people to remember His works by writing them down, telling them to their children, or setting a visual reminder.

When we record what God has done—whether in a journal, on a notecard, or even in our phone's notes—we create a trail of testimony. When doubt whispers in our ears or trials hit us hard, we can look back and see His faithfulness written in our own handwriting. It's proof to ourselves and a witness to others that God is with us.

Writing it down is a way to treasure what God has done. It keeps our hearts steady in gratitude and truth. What will you write down today?

SPEAK LIFE: "Writing down what God has done helps me remember His faithfulness."

TALK TO GOD: Lord, show me how You want me to record Your works in my life. Amen.

REFLECT & RESPOND: What's one way God has been faithful to you? Write it down today so you can remember later.

DAY 335

Reflect

Take a few moments to revisit the days you've just walked. There's no rush here—just honesty and grace. Feel free to journal your answers.

Reflection Prompts:

- ✓ What truth stood out to me this week?
- ✓ Where did I notice God inviting me to stop settling?
- ✓ What challenged me? What encouraged me?
- ✓ What thought/encouragement/hope do I want to carry with me into the coming days?

DAY 336

Rest

Today is a day to rest—not to catch up, fix something, or prove anything. Abundant life includes stopping long enough to receive what God is already offering you.

Sit quietly with God for a few minutes.

Breathe deeply.

Allow any Scripture from the past few days to encourage you.

Let yourself be loved and cared for by your Creator.

DAY 337

Turn to Him First

"This is what the Sovereign Lord, the Holy One of Israel, says: 'Only in returning to me and resting in me will you be saved. In quietness and confidence is your strength ...'"

Isaiah 30:15a NLT

Who do you run to for help first?

We may turn to a family member, a friend, or even to an online search engine for help. Isaiah warned the people of Judah not to turn to foreign powers in their need, but rather to God. This message is timely for us today, too.

When we face troubles and tribulations in life, instead of turning to worldly solutions or to the influence of others, God reminds us that in Him we find salvation and strength—everything we need. The world cannot give us what God can. Returning to God and His ways allows us to rest in His perfect timing, to experience His peace, and to find confidence in His power and promises.

The next time trouble comes knocking on your door, remember Who to turn to first. You're in good hands, friend.

SPEAK LIFE: "When troubles come, I turn to God first."

TALK TO GOD: Lord God, remind me to turn to You first in all situations in my life. You are all I need. Amen.

REFLECT & RESPOND: Where have you sought help lately? What would it look like to seek the Lord in your need instead?

DAY 338

Reject the Pressure to Prove

"For it is by grace you have been saved, through faith—and this is not from yourselves, it is the gift of God—not by works, so that no one can boast."

Ephesians 2:8-9 NIV

When have you recently felt the pressure to prove your worth?

The world constantly pushes us to measure up—by success, appearance, productivity, or even spiritual performance. This quiet, never-ending pressure can leave us exhausted, always striving and never settled.

Ephesians declares a freeing truth. Your salvation—and your worth—are a gift of God's grace. They are not earned, achieved, or maintained by effort. You don't belong to God because you performed well enough; you belong to Him because of His grace.

This grace silences that inner voice that beckons, "Do more. Be more." It replaces striving with stillness and pressure with peace.

Today, release the need to prove anything. Rest in what God has already declared true: you are saved by grace, held by love, and secure in Him—right where you are.

SPEAK LIFE: "God's grace is all I need. I don't have to prove anything."

TALK TO GOD: Lord, when I feel the pressure to prove I am worthy and enough, continue to remind me Your grace is all I need. Amen.

REFLECT & RESPOND: Where do you feel the most pressure to prove yourself today? How might you invite God's peace into that area?

DAY 339

Echo God, Not the Enemy

"He has always hated the truth, because there is no truth in him. When he lies, it is consistent with his character; for he is a liar and the father of lies."

John 8:44b NLT

Whose words are you echoing?

The enemy of our souls is loud, relentless, and deceitful. His lies attempt to keep us afraid, ashamed, or stuck. They only have power if we repeat them, if we echo his words over our lives. When we make statements like, "I'll never have enough. I can't change. God doesn't love me," we magnify his lies.

John makes it clear. This enemy, the devil, is the father of lies. Nothing he says can be trusted. God has already spoken His truth over us, so why would we listen to the enemy's words? When we repeat God's truth—out loud, in prayer, and in daily declarations— the enemy's lies are silenced, and our faith flourishes.

Don't echo the enemy today. Echo God. Speak His Word. Proclaim His promises. The only voice worth magnifying is the Voice of Truth Himself.

SPEAK LIFE: "Echoing the truth of God silences the lies of the enemy."

TALK TO GOD: Lord, guide me to replace the enemy's lies with Your truth. Help me to echo You. Amen.

REFLECT & RESPOND: What lie from the enemy are you repeating today? How might your life look different if you echoed God's truth instead?

DAY 340

Change the Atmosphere with Your Words

"Let your conversation be always full of grace, seasoned with salt, so that you may know how to answer everyone."

Colossians 4:6 NIV

Have you ever experienced how a timely word of encouragement can almost instantly revive someone's weary soul? Or how a kind reply can turn a harsh conversation into a peaceful one?

God's Word reminds us to let our words be full of grace and seasoned with salt—not bland, but rather life-giving and preserving.

Think about the last time you experienced a shift in the atmosphere because of what was spoken. Maybe laughter broke the heaviness, an apology brought restoration, or someone's gentle affirmation reminded you that you weren't alone. Words hold this kind of power.

As followers of Jesus, we're called to use our voices to never tear down, but instead to build up, to bring God's light into dark spaces. Every room you enter, whether at home, at work, or online, is an opportunity to change the atmosphere. When you choose grace-filled words, you invite God's presence into the moment. His presence changes everything.

SPEAK LIFE: "My words matter. They can change the atmosphere."

TALK TO GOD: Lord God, please give me Your life-giving and preserving words today. Amen.

REFLECT & RESPOND: When have your words either calmed or escalated the atmosphere recently? How is God inviting you to speak words of life today?

DAY 341

Allow God to Redeem Your Past

"'Forget the former things; do not dwell on the past. See, I am doing a new thing! Now it springs up; do you not perceive it? I am making a way in the wilderness and streams in the wasteland ...'"

Isaiah 43:18-19 NIV

Do you ever feel stuck in who you used to be?

The enemy would love to keep you reliving old habits and past mistakes so you won't dare step into abundance.

Through the prophet Isaiah, God proclaims to forget the former things. You are not your former self, because God is doing a new thing. This new thing? It's you. He's restoring you, refining you, and freeing you. He's redeemed you by name and is equipping you to grow in grace.

You're not stuck in yesterday's story. Your past is part of your journey, yes, but it doesn't get to write your future. Allow God to bring beauty from the past, and make rivers in your former wasteland.

Take a breath. Know you're not who you used to be. You're becoming who He's always seen you to be—whole, dearly loved, and free.

SPEAK LIFE: "God is doing something new in me."

TALK TO GOD: Lord, continue to do the work of molding me into the woman You desire for me to be. Amen.

REFLECT & RESPOND: What "former thing" are you dwelling on? Surrender it to God, and perceive the new thing He's doing in you.

DAY 342

Reflect

Take a few moments to revisit the days you've just walked. There's no rush here—just honesty and grace. Feel free to journal your answers.

Reflection Prompts:

- ✓ What truth stood out to me this week?
- ✓ Where did I notice God inviting me to stop settling?
- ✓ What challenged me? What encouraged me?
- ✓ What thought/encouragement/hope do I want to carry with me into the coming days?

DAY 343

Rest

Today is a day to rest—not to catch up, fix something, or prove anything. Abundant life includes stopping long enough to receive what God is already offering you.

Sit quietly with God for a few minutes.

Breathe deeply.

Allow any Scripture from the past few days to encourage you.

Let yourself be loved and cared for by your Creator.

DAY 344

Bless with Your Unique Gifts

"God has given each of you a gift from his great variety of spiritual gifts. Use them well to serve one another."

1 Peter 4:10 NLT

Do you realize how your contribution to the world around you is wonderfully unique?

Peter reminds us that every gift God gives is purposeful. He has gifted you with a unique combination of talents, experiences, and heart that can bless others in ways no one else can. Your gifting is specifically for you, and you're the only one who can give the way you do.

Your gift might be your sense of humor that brings light to a weary friend, your ability to listen that calms a stressed soul, or your creativity that inspires hope in one who is struggling. The more you bless others with your gifts, the better their lives become, and the more God is glorified.

When you embrace your individuality in giving, you reflect God's grace in ways only you can. Remember today that your contribution is unique. God can multiply your gifts to bless others in extraordinary ways.

SPEAK LIFE: "God created me with unique gifts which I use to bless others."

TALK TO GOD: Lord, guide me to use my God-given unique gifts to bless and serve others. Amen.

REFLECT & RESPOND: What's one way you can serve others with your unique gifts today? How will you thank God for these gifts?

DAY 345

Stand Firm for God

"Peter and the other apostles replied: 'We must obey God rather than human beings! …'"

Acts 5:29 NIV

When was the last time following God cost you something?

Peter and the apostles were examples of standing in conviction when tested. Faced with opposition, they chose to obey God rather than give in to fear or the pressure of others. Their courage came from trusting that God's authority outweighed anyone else's.

Obeying God over others isn't easy or popular. It may mean standing alone, choosing truth over comfort, or quietly refusing to compromise your integrity. Yet, this kind of faithfulness reveals where your loyalty truly lies—grounded in the One Who created you, calls you, and sustains you.

When you stand firm for God, you reflect Jesus to a watching world. Your courage may inspire others to do the same. Even if no one else sees, God does, and He delights in your obedience.

SPEAK LIFE: "I will obey God over others today, even if it's unpopular."

TALK TO GOD: Lord, help me to always stand up for what is right, not what is popular. Give me the courage to trust You in the isolating situations of life. Amen.

REFLECT & RESPOND: Where might God be calling you to stand firm amid opposition? How can you rely on His strength when the pressure to conform is strong?

DAY 346

Live Ready for His Return

"You also must be ready all the time, for the Son of Man will come when least expected."

Matthew 24:44 NLT

How ready are you for Jesus' return?

Jesus reminds us through Matthew that His return does contain a countdown. There will be no notifications or alerts that He is almost here. Instead, He will come when we least expect Him. Consequently, we are called to live in a state of readiness: alert, watchful, and faithful in the everyday moments of life.

Being ready means living in a manner that if Jesus returned this very moment, we would be found walking closely with Him—loving, forgiving, serving, and shining His light into this world. It's being prepared, and not succumbing to fear or anxiety about the unknown.

When our hope is secure in Jesus' promised return, we view our days differently. Temporary distractions become insignificant. Petty arguments seem small. Faithfulness in the small things is suddenly extra important and meaningful.

Being ready is less about waiting and more about walking—steadily, faithfully, daily—with Him.

SPEAK LIFE: "Today I live prepared for Jesus' return."

TALK TO GOD: God, I want to be ready for when Jesus returns. Guide me to walk closely with Him—today and every day. Amen.

REFLECT & RESPOND: What is distracting you from living ready for Jesus' return? How can you begin to prepare yourself today?

DAY 347

Realize You are Loved

"O Lord, you have examined my heart and know everything about me. You know when I sit down or stand up. You know my thoughts even when I'm far away."

Psalm 139:1-2 NLT

Do you ever feel the need to keep explaining yourself, clarifying what you mean or trying to be understood?

You might feel this way with others, but you never have to explain yourself to God. He already knows. Every thought you think, every emotion you feel, every moment you experience—He's been with you through it all. You are fully known, and still, deeply loved.

King David declared how God knew everything about him, and He knows everything about you, too. He knows the longings of your heart, the weight of your worries, the hopes you hold, and the dreams to which you quietly cling. God's aware of all of it—and all of you.

He doesn't flinch at your failures or mock your fears. He is with you through it all, and He carries you with care. You are known and loved, just as you are.

SPEAK LIFE: "God knows me and loves me fully."

TALK TO GOD: Lord, help me remember that You know me and love me, just as I am. Amen.

REFLECT & RESPOND: Where do you doubt that God sees you with love? Write it down, and ask God to meet you in this doubt today.

DAY 348

Choose Obedience Over Outcome

"But Samuel replied: 'Does the Lord delight in burnt offerings and sacrifices as much as in obeying the Lord? To obey is better than sacrifice, and to heed is better than the fat of rams ...'"

1 Samuel 15:22 NIV

Do you ever fixate on the outcome of your circumstances?

Samuel's words to King Saul remind us of a powerful truth: obeying is better than offering sacrifices. Sometimes we desire certain results, but God values our obedience more than the outcome itself.

Obedience means trusting God's instructions and walking in His ways, even when we don't fully understand the plan or see immediate results. It's about faithfulness to God rather than chasing after our own desires or measuring success by our accomplishments.

When you choose obedience, you're aligning yourself with God's best. The outcomes, whether big or small, will follow in God's perfect timing. Your faithful steps, even when uncertain, please Him and build a foundation for future blessings.

Obeying God isn't always easy, but it is always worth it. Trust that He is leading you toward what's best—one obedient step at a time.

SPEAK LIFE: "No matter what, I choose to obey God today."

TALK TO GOD: God, guide my heart and will to obey You, no matter how uncomfortable it may feel. Amen.

REFLECT & RESPOND: How is God calling you to obey today? How can you practice faithfulness by trusting God's leading?

DAY 349

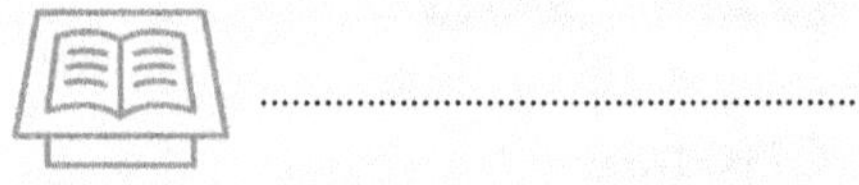

Reflect

Take a few moments to revisit the days you've just walked. There's no rush here—just honesty and grace. Feel free to journal your answers.

Reflection Prompts:

- ✓ What truth stood out to me this week?
- ✓ Where did I notice God inviting me to stop settling?
- ✓ What challenged me? What encouraged me?
- ✓ What thought/encouragement/hope do I want to carry with me into the coming days?

DAY 350

Rest

Today is a day to rest—not to catch up, fix something, or prove anything. Abundant life includes stopping long enough to receive what God is already offering you.

Sit quietly with God for a few minutes.

Breathe deeply.

Allow any Scripture from the past few days to encourage you.

Let yourself be loved and cared for by your Creator.

DAY 351

Live in the Overflow of Grace

"From his abundance we have all received one gracious blessing after another."

John 1:16 NLT

Have you ever questioned how God's grace works?

John reminds us that from Jesus' abundance, we receive grace upon grace—one blessing after another. It's not given sparingly, nor is it a drip or a trickle. It's a steady overflow of God's unearned favor, and His supply never runs dry.

Think of ocean waves. One rolls in, and before it fades, another follows. That's how God's grace works. Yesterday's grace carried you through yesterday, and today's grace is already here to meet you today. Tomorrow? More grace is on the way because His abundance never ends.

Grace is God's undeserved kindness. It forgives when you fail, strengthens when you're weak, and sustains when you're weary. You don't have to earn it; just simply receive it. As His grace flows in you, it also flows through you, empowering you to extend the same grace to others.

Embrace this truth today: you are living in the overflow of God's grace.

SPEAK LIFE: "I am living in the overflow of God's grace."

TALK TO GOD: Lord, thank You for Your amazing grace. Empower me to live in it and to extend it to others. Amen.

REFLECT & RESPOND: When has God's grace encouraged you recently? How can you extend that same grace to someone else today?

DAY 352

Choose to Be Still

"'… The Lord will fight for you; you need only to be still.'"

Exodus 14:14 NIV

Is doing nothing the hardest thing for you to do?

Oftentimes, our instinct is to rush in, fix, defend, or control. God, however, has a counterintuitive invitation: be still.

Stillness isn't passive, as we might think. Nor is it giving up or a sign of weakness. It's simply choosing to trust that God is already at work on your behalf, even when you can't see it yet. The Israelites stood on the edge of the Red Sea with Pharaoh's army closing in, and God told them to be still. Not run. Not hide. Not fight. Just stand and watch.

Choosing to be still means allowing God to be God, without any action on our part. It means resting in who He says He is, remaining confident that He fights for, defends, and protects us in His perfect sovereignty.

Friend, you don't need to fix it or control it. Simply be still, and trust Him.

SPEAK LIFE: "Instead of trying to fix it, I choose to be still and trust God."

TALK TO GOD: God, when I want to fix or control the situation, help me to be still and trust You instead. Amen.

REFLECT & RESPOND: Where do you feel pressure to act now instead of waiting? How can you practice stillness and trust God instead?

DAY 353

Invite God's Rest

"Then, because so many people were coming and going that they did not even have a chance to eat, he said to them, 'Come with me by yourselves to a quiet place and get some rest.'"

Mark 6:31 NIV

Do you ever view rest negatively?

We sometimes see it as unproductive, indulgent, or even lazy. Mark shows us that Jesus' example of rest is essential, not optional. Jesus understood the importance of stepping away from life's demands to reconnect with His Father, regain strength, and refocus on the important.

If Jesus can rest, so can you. This deliberate act of self-care and following God's rhythm isn't something to feel guilty or ashamed about. Taking time to rest doesn't mean you're falling behind or wasting your day. It's essential for an abundant life.

When you rest, you're not running from your duties. You're running to God. You're creating space for Him to speak, refresh, and guide you. Invite this vital rhythm of God's timing and provision into your life. It may be the most powerful thing you do all week.

SPEAK LIFE: "Rest is essential for my well-being and my relationship with God."

TALK TO GOD: Lord, show me where I can intentionally rest with You this week. Amen.

REFLECT & RESPOND: Where in your week could you rest with God? How might that strengthen your life and relationship with Him?

DAY 354

Train Your Eyes to See

"So we fix our eyes not on what is seen, but on what is unseen, since what is seen is temporary, but what is unseen is eternal."

2 Corinthians 4:18 NIV

What do you see today?

The challenges, the frustrations, and the disappointments are easy to notice. Our physical eyes are designed to view what's visible, but faith calls us to something better. Paul reminds us that everything we see now is temporary. The true treasures—the eternal ones—are often unseen.

Training your spiritual sight is like adjusting the lens on a camera. At first, the picture may be blurry, but as you focus, what's eternal becomes clearer: God's faithfulness, His promises, and His unseen work. When your eyes are fixed on the eternal, your heart is steady—no matter what.

Today, lift your gaze. Refuse to let your perspective be limited to right now. Instead, look through the eyes of faith to see what's eternal. That's the vision that transforms how you live today.

SPEAK LIFE: "I focus on what's eternal, not on what I see now."

TALK TO GOD: God, shift my gaze to see things from Your perspective and Your eternal view. Amen.

REFLECT & RESPOND: What's one unseen truth from God's Word you can focus on today? Who else in your life needs this perspective shift?

DAY 355

Live Chosen, Not Chasing

"Even before he made the world, God loved us and chose us in Christ to be holy and without fault in his eyes. God decided in advance to adopt us into his own family by bringing us to himself through Jesus Christ. This is what he wanted to do, and it gave him great pleasure."

Ephesians 1:4-5 NLT

Do you ever forget that you are God's chosen daughter?

A thief of contentment is the constant chasing after approval, belonging, and worth. It's almost as if what we chase is always just out of our reach.

God's Word declares that you don't have to chase what you already have. Get this: before the world began, God chose you. He loved you, called you His own, and delighted to make you part of His family.

This truth affects how you live. You no longer need to chase after what others think or scramble to prove yourself. You can stand firm, deeply grounded in the reality that you are chosen and loved. This, right here, is true contentment.

SPEAK LIFE: "God chose me, and I have nothing to chase."

TALK TO GOD: God, thank You for choosing me. Sink this reality deep in my heart, and equip me to live it out. Amen.

REFLECT & RESPOND: What are you tempted to chase today? How can you rest in the truth that God has already chosen you?

DAY 356

Reflect

Take a few moments to revisit the days you've just walked. There's no rush here—just honesty and grace. Feel free to journal your answers.

Reflection Prompts:

- ✓ What truth stood out to me this week?
- ✓ Where did I notice God inviting me to stop settling?
- ✓ What challenged me? What encouraged me?
- ✓ What thought/encouragement/hope do I want to carry with me into the coming days?

DAY 357

Rest

Today is a day to rest—not to catch up, fix something, or prove anything. Abundant life includes stopping long enough to receive what God is already offering you.

Sit quietly with God for a few minutes.

Breathe deeply.

Allow any Scripture from the past few days to encourage you.

Let yourself be loved and cared for by your Creator.

DAY 358

Honor One Another

"Be devoted to one another in love. Honor one another above yourselves."

Romans 12:10 NIV

How well do you honor others, especially above yourself?

Paul's instruction is clear. Love one another and honor others above yourself. Yet, this can be challenging, can't it? Honoring others requires humility and intention. When we put the needs and desires of others before our own, we value them. When we pause to notice, listen, and care when we don't feel like it, we live out God's love. When we seek another's best interest first, we follow the example of Jesus.

Jesus modeled this perfectly. Biblical example after example, we see how He loved unconditionally and consistently placed others above Himself. He spoke words of life, ministered to the hurting, and reached out to the lost—all for their good and God's glory. He calls us to do the same.

Today, ask God to show you specific ways to honor someone above yourself. As you do, not only will others be blessed, but your heart will be reminded of all Jesus has done for you.

SPEAK LIFE: "Today, I will honor others above myself."

TALK TO GOD: God, who can I love well and honor today? Open my eyes and guide me. Amen.

REFLECT & RESPOND: Who in your life could use some love right now? How can you honor this person above yourself?

DAY 359

Speak Life Over Your Future

"'… For I know the plans I have for you,' says the Lord. 'They are plans for good and not for disaster, to give you a future and a hope …'"

Jeremiah 29:11 NLT

When you think about the future, do you ever wander into worry or "what ifs"?

What if things don't work out? What if I can't do it? God reminds us that our future is secure in His hands, and He has goodness and hope planned for us.

The words you speak about your tomorrow shape how you walk into it today. When you declare God's promises instead of your fears, you align yourself with His truth. Instead of saying, "I don't know if I'll ever get through this," you can try, "God is leading me and has good plans for me."

Speaking life over your future isn't wishful thinking. It's partnering with God in the hope-filled story He's written for your life. Every word of faith you speak today sows seeds of promise into the days ahead.

SPEAK LIFE: "I speak hope because my future is secure in God's hands."

TALK TO GOD: Lord, guide my words to be filled with Your hope and promises for my future. Amen.

REFLECT & RESPOND: Have you been speaking fear-filled or faith-filled words about your future? Write down three of God's promises to declare over your life.

DAY 360

Pour Out and Be Filled

"'… Give, and you will receive. Your gift will return to you in full—pressed down, shaken together to make room for more, running over, and poured into your lap. The amount you give will determine the amount you get back.'"

Luke 6:38 NLT

Does the fear of depleting your time, resources, or love ever keep you from giving lavishly?

Jesus reminds us that the more we give, the more He fills us. This isn't a plan for earning blessings, but rather a promise that when we live with a giving heart, God blesses us beyond our imaginations.

Each act of giving releases God's favor in our lives and in others'. This favor opens the door for God's presence to be lavishly poured back into us.

The truth is this: you can never outgive God. The more you give and pour out, the more you will receive from Him. So, go ahead and give lavishly today, and watch how He fills you with more than you could ever ask or imagine.

SPEAK LIFE: "I give lavishly, knowing God will fill me and provide my needs."

TALK TO GOD: Lord, show me today how I can give lavishly to others. I trust You will fill me to overflowing. Amen.

REFLECT & RESPOND: What is one small thing you can give today that might bless someone else? How have you recently seen God fill you up after giving?

DAY 361

Answer God's Call

"And the Lord came and called as before, 'Samuel! Samuel!' And Samuel replied, 'Speak, your servant is listening.'"

1 Samuel 3:10 NLT

When have you been surprised by God's call?

His call may seem as if it's coming out of nowhere. It may feel startling or inconvenient. Samuel might have understood this. He was just a boy when he heard the Lord's voice, yet his simple response to God saying he was listening changed the course of his life and the lives of an entire nation.

Sometimes, God asks something small; other times, it feels enormous. The important piece here isn't the size of the task, but rather the willingness of your heart. Saying yes to God's call can open doors, shift your direction, and set in motion God's purposes in ways you could never anticipate.

What seems ordinary or small to you can be extraordinary in God's hands. Trust that when you respond to His call, you are stepping into a story only He can write. Your positive response is enough, and it can change everything.

SPEAK LIFE: "When God calls me, I will listen and positively respond."

TALK TO GOD: Lord, when You call me, prompt me to answer immediately. Use my "yes" according to Your will. Amen.

REFLECT & RESPOND: In what way is God calling you today? How will you step forward in obedience, trusting God will bless your response?

DAY 362

Put God's Kingdom First

"But seek first his kingdom and his righteousness, and all these things will be given to you as well."

Matthew 6:33 NIV

Do you ever get caught up in what feels urgent?

Much of life seems in need of our immediate attention. Deadlines at work. Kids' schedules. Bills to pay. Meals to plan. Our days can feel like a never-ending shuffle of tasks and priorities. Sadly, God and His kingdom can slip down the priority list without us even realizing it.

Jesus flips our perspective, though. He says to put God's kingdom first, and everything else will find its place. This is about aligning ourselves with God and seeking His best. When we prioritize His ways, His will, and His righteousness, life doesn't necessarily get easier, but it does get more orderly. Peace replaces pressure, and clarity overrides chaos.

This kingdom-first living is a daily choice. It's choosing prayer over panic, obedience over convenience, and eternal treasure over temporary things. It's living today with an eternal view. Begin every decision today with this question: *How does this align with God and His kingdom?*

SPEAK LIFE: "Today, I seek God and His kingdom first."

TALK TO GOD: Lord God, prompt me to seek You and Your kingdom ahead of anything else, trusting You in every way. Amen.

REFLECT & RESPOND: What competes most with God in your daily priorities? How can you realign your focus to put Him first today?

DAY 363

Embrace His New Mercies

"The faithful love of the Lord never ends! His mercies never cease. Great is his faithfulness; his mercies begin afresh each morning."

Lamentations 3:22-23 NLT

Could you use some of God's mercy today?

Every sunrise reminds us of God's faithfulness. When the world wakes, His mercies are new again—not recycled or leftover, but rather fresh grace for a brand-new day.

Maybe yesterday felt messy. Maybe you stumbled, spoke harshly, or carried regret into the night. You don't need to drag yesterday's failures into today. God's mercy met you even before you opened your eyes.

Mercy is God's compassion in our weakness. Thankfully, He doesn't treat us as our sins deserve, but He offers forgiveness and kindness we could never earn. His mercy is never-ending because His love is never-ending. No matter how many times we've needed it before, there is still more mercy today.

Because of this, you can step into today with confidence and peace. His mercy covers yesterday, sustains today, and carries you into tomorrow.

Take a deep breath. The slate is clean. His mercies are new—again.

SPEAK LIFE: "God's mercies are new for me today."

TALK TO GOD: God, thank You for Your new mercies. Help me to step into today with Your confidence and peace. Amen.

REFLECT & RESPOND: Where in your life could you use God's mercy right now? Pause to thank Him for the gift of a new day and a clean slate.

DAY 364

Reflect

Take a few moments to revisit the days you've just walked. There's no rush here—just honesty and grace. Feel free to journal your answers.

Reflection Prompts:

- ✓ What truth stood out to me this week?
- ✓ Where did I notice God inviting me to stop settling?
- ✓ What challenged me? What encouraged me?
- ✓ What thought/encouragement/hope do I want to carry with me into the coming days?

DAY 365

Rest

Today is a day to rest—not to catch up, fix something, or prove anything. Abundant life includes stopping long enough to receive what God is already offering you.

Sit quietly with God for a few minutes.

Breathe deeply.

Allow any Scripture from the past few days to encourage you.

Let yourself be loved and cared for by your Creator.

A FINAL BLESSING

As you come to the end of these pages, please know how proud I am of you. Not for finishing a book, but rather for choosing to keep showing up for your abundant life through Jesus.

Whether you read every day, skipped some days, lingered on others, or started again—maybe more than once—what matters is that you kept returning. Every return matters to God.

May you keep noticing His presence in ordinary moments.

May you hear His voice more clearly than that of pressure or fear.

May you rest when you need to rest and move when He invites you to move.

May your life feel less rushed and more grounded.

May you remember, again and again, that you were never made to settle.

And when you forget, because we all do, may God gently remind you that He is near, He is faithful, and He continues to offer you life in abundance.

You don't walk forward alone.

He goes with you.

And so do my prayers.

Julie

ACKNOWLEDGMENTS

First, to Jesus. Thank You for meeting me in my mess and for saving my soul. I am forever grateful for You and Your love. Thank You for showing me there's more to life than settling for less than Your best through embracing the abundant life You came to give. Thank You for Your discernment, guidance, presence, and provision in every aspect of this book. It would not exist without You. I love living life as an adventure with You!

To Bill. Thank you for loving me steadily, believing in me, and supporting the calling God has placed on my life. Thank you for your patience through the long hours, the full seasons, and the many moments when I was writing, thinking, editing, and dreaming. I thank God for you, and I love you forever.

To Alissa, Morgan, Nolan, Griffin, Zach, Paige, and Jade. Thank you for the blessings that you are to me. I love the special bond we share. Thank you for always reminding me what truly matters in life. You are some of the greatest gifts God has given me, and I love you more than you know. Thank you for loving me.

To Tina. Thank you for your wisdom, your care, and your commitment to helping me bring this message to life. Thank you for cheering me on, sharpening my words, and walking beside me through every stage of this process. I couldn't have done this without you.

To Nelly. Thank you for taking what was in my heart and helping me bring it to life visually. Thank you for your creativity, professionalism, and attention to detail. Your work helped turn this devotional into something beautiful, clear, and ready to hold in a reader's hands.

To the women I serve through the Encouragement for Real Life Podcast, Abundant Life Mentoring, speaking events, and everyday conversations. Thank you for sharing your stories and for entrusting them to me. You and they matter. Your honesty matters. Your courage matters. You are the reason I keep showing up. You've reminded me again and again that numerous women love God deeply and still feel tired, distracted, and stretched thin. This book is for you. My prayer is that these pages help you breathe again, hear Jesus more clearly, and remember that you were never made to settle.

You were made for more.

ABOUT THE AUTHOR

 **Julie Lefebure** is a writer, speaker, and mentor who helps women live with intention and experience the abundant life God promises. She is the author of *Right Now Matters* and *Right Now Matters Bible Study*, and the host of the *Encouragement for Real Life Podcast*, where she shares honest stories, biblical truths, and practical encouragement for everyday faith.

Julie's heart is to walk with women who love God but sometimes feel weary, distracted, or stuck going through the motions. Through her writing, mentoring, events, and resources, she invites women to slow down, listen to God's voice, and live from His truth—rather than from pressure, comparison, or fear.

She is the founder of Abundant Life Mentoring and loves creating spaces where women can breathe, be seen, and be reminded of who they are in Christ.

Julie lives in Iowa with her husband and treasures time with her family, especially being "Monna" to her three grandchildren. She loves quiet mornings, meaningful conversations, sunrises and sunsets, and reminding women everywhere that they were never made to settle—they were made for more.

You can find more from Julie and access the Made for More free resources at julielefebure.com/resources.